LIBERTY: LEGACY OF TRUTH

*To those young in spirit who are ever
seeking an improved understanding of
liberty and its countless blessings.*

OTHER BOOKS BY LEONARD E. READ

Romance of Reality (o.p.)
Pattern for Revolt
Instead of Violence
Outlook for Freedom (o.p.)
Government: An Ideal Concept
   Governo Um Concito Ideal
Why Not Try Freedom?
   ¿Por Que No Ensayar la Libertad?
Elements of Libertarian Leadership
Anything That's Peaceful
   Todo Por la Paz
The Free Market and its Enemy
   El Enemigo del Mercado Libre
Deeper Than You Think
Accent on the Right
The Coming Aristocracy
Let Freedom Reign
Talking to Myself
Then Truth Will Out
To Free or Freeze
Who's Listening?
Having My Way
Castles In The Air
The Love of Liberty
Comes the Dawn
Awake for Freedom's Sake
Vision

LEONARD E. READ

LIBERTY: LEGACY OF TRUTH

The Foundation for Economic Education, Inc.
Irvington-on-Hudson, New York 10533
1978

THE AUTHOR AND PUBLISHER

Leonard E. Read has been president of The Foundation for Economic Education since it was organized in 1946.

The Foundation is a nonpolitical, nonprofit, educational institution. Its senior staff and numerous writers are students as well as teachers of the free market, private ownership, limited government rationale. Sample copies of the Foundation's monthly study journal, *The Freeman,* are available on request.

Published September 1978

ISBN-0-910614-60-1

Printed in U.S.A.

CONTENTS

1

LIBERTY: LEGACY OF TRUTH

There are three parts to truth: first the inquiry, which is the wooing of it; secondly, the knowledge of it, which is the presence of it; and thirdly, the belief, which is the enjoyment of it.
—FRANCIS BACON

As Plutarch wrote, "To make no mistakes is not in the power of man; but from these errors and mistakes the wise and good learn wisdom for the future."

Francis Bacon (1561-1626), active in political affairs during the reigns of Queen Elizabeth and James I, had his share of errors and mistakes. However, he learned from his mistakes and achieved renown as a philosopher and statesman. Obviously, not to err is beyond finite man's power, but the capability of moving toward truth is within man's range. Bacon, after becoming a philosopher and statesman—wise and good—bequeathed to us a remarkable three-part formula.

I. The wooing of truth—One's ambition in every laudable endeavor should be nothing less than an ever-improving excellence. Perpetual inquiry is the only way to this

1

objective—the wooing of truth. As Cicero wrote, "It is a shameful thing to be weary of inquiry when what we search for is excellent."

The wooing of truth presupposes a growth in awareness, perception, consciousness. It is founded on individual emergence or evolution. Dr. Robert A. Millikan, that great physicist and for years Chairman of the California Institute of Technology, was graced with an inquiring mind. He wrote:

> Three ideas stand out above all others in the influence they have exerted and are destined to exert upon the development of the human race: the idea of the Golden Rule, the idea of natural law, and the idea of age-long growth, or *evolution*.

The Golden Rule, doubtless the wisest of all moral maxims, was first recorded by Confucius four centuries prior to Christianity: "Do not unto others what you would not they should do unto you." Since then, it has been adopted with slightly different phrasings by nine of the world's leading religions.

The Golden Rule embodies the principle of universality, and thus is a guide to sorting good from evil. Example: Does anyone have the right to take the life, the livelihood, the liberty of another? No, because this is not a "right" that can be conceded to all others. It is evil! Reflect on the opposite principle: I have the right to my life, my livelihood, my liberty. Can I concede this right to all earthly beings? I can! Therefore, it is good!

What is meant by the Natural Law, sometimes called the Higher Law—an ideal of justice superior to the decrees of those in power? This ideal, discoverable but not invented by reason, is the ground for declaring that something may be legal, but also unjust. This is to say that Power, whether wielded by dictocrats or "the people," never is the last word. The last word rests with an ideal of righteousness written into the ultimate nature of things, binding our governors and governed alike.

Evolution is attuned to Natural Law. Individuals who are responsive to this Heavenly radiation, instead of growing weary of inquiry, look upon successive moments of their mortal lives as opening up new and exciting opportunities. Their aim is to grow toward the ideal—Truth. But achieve the Ultimate? Never! Evolution is not an end, but a process of growth. Human destiny is emergence—now and forever!

II. The Knowledge of Truth—Many people in today's world have no better awareness of truth than to confuse it with a mere nose count: "The majority is always right." What an affront to knowledge! As one sage remarked, "It is twice as hard to crush a half-truth as a whole lie." And it is far easier to find countless persons who know some truth than to find one among them knowledgeable enough, in the face of opposition, to stand for it. With these thoughts in mind, here are several wise observations on the foundation of truth—knowledge:

- The first step to knowledge is to know we are ignorant.
  —*Richard Cecil*

- Knowledge is the eye of desire and *can* become the pilot of the soul. —*Will Durant*

- He that would make real progress in knowledge, must dedicate his age as well as youth . . . at the altar of truth.   —*George Berkeley*

- Man is not born to solve the problem of the universe, but to find out what he has to do; and to restrain himself within the limits of his comprehension. —*Goethe*

- Real knowledge, like everything of value, is not to be obtained easily. It must be worked for, studied for, thought for and, more than all, must be prayed for.
                                    —*Thomas A. Arnold*

- All wish to possess knowledge, but few, comparatively speaking, are willing to pay the price.   —*Juvenal*

- I had six honest serving men
  They taught me all I knew;
  Their names were Where and What and When
  And Why and How and Who.   —*Kipling*

III. The enjoyment of truth—"Those who would enjoyment gain must find in it the purpose they pursue." Those who succeed in their pursuit of truth find a glorious enjoyment in its revelation: freedom to act creatively as they please! As written in John 8:32, *"The truth shall make you free."* And it does!

Let us assess another revealing wisdom bequeathed to mankind many centuries ago:

But whosoever looketh into the perfect law of liberty, and continueth therein, he being not a forgetful hearer, but a doer of the work, this man shall be blessed in his deed.—James 1:25

The nearest approach to the perfect law of liberty began in 1776—born of a truth never before expressed in a political document: *Man's rights to life and livelihood are endowed by the Creator.* Government removed from the role of endower!

Those of us "who would enjoyment gain" were given the guidelines by Saint James:

- Look into the perfect law of liberty and continue to do so—now and always.
- Never forget what is learned as so many do, but be "a doer of the work."
- This man—the doer—"shall be blessed in his deed" and live a life of enjoyment.

May more and more of us understand Bacon's three parts to truth and live by them. *The legacy is liberty!*

***

Wondering how I might introduce the following chapters, I came upon some observations by Samuel Ullman in his book, *From the Summit of Years Four Score.* His reflections and mine on the 80th year of our lives are surprisingly similar:

Youth is not a time of life; it is a state of mind; it is not a matter of rosy cheeks, red lips and supple knees; it is a matter of the will, a quality of the imagination, a vigor of the emotions; it is the freshness of the deep springs of life.

Youth means the predominance of courage over timidity, of adventure over the love of ease. This often exists in a man of sixty more than in a boy of twenty. Nobody grows old merely by a number of years. We grow old by deserting our ideals.

Years may wrinkle the skin, but to give up enthusiasm wrinkles the soul. Worry, doubt, self-distrust, fear and despair—these bow the heart and turn the spirit back to dust.

Whether sixty or sixteen, there is in every human being's heart the love of wonder, the sweet amazement at the stars and the starlike things, the undaunted challenge of events, the unfailing child-like appetite for what-next, and the joy of the game of living.

You are as young as your faith, as old as your doubt; as young as your self-confidence, as old as your fear; as young as your hope, as old as your despair.

Hail to the young!

2

FAITH: THE LEAVEN
OF LIBERTY

Faith makes the discords of the
present the harmonies of the fu-
ture.   **—ROBERT COLLYER**

Wrote Alexis de Tocqueville, "Despotism may govern without faith, but Liberty cannot." The millions of despots, now in the driver's seat, are swayed not by faith but by that type of ignorance displayed by witch doctors or medicine men and their patients. They, who do not know how to run their own lives, do not know that they know not how to run the lives of others.

There are countless forms of ignorance which no individual—past or present—has overcome. But there is no form more disharmonious or destructive than despotism. Can despots govern without faith? Affirmative! For confirmation, have a look at history and today's world—here and elsewhere.

Is faith, really, the leaven of liberty? Goethe shares two wise observations:

- Epochs of faith are epochs of fruitfulness; but epochs of unbelief, however glittering, are barren of all permanent good.
- Miracle is the darling child of faith.

Liberty—no man-concocted restraints against the release of creative energy—can be likened to a bright star in a dark firmament. Only now and then in all history has that star brightened the lives of the trillions who have inhabited this earth. In view of the fact that he who believes is strong and he who doubts is weak, it behooves us to strengthen our belief in the role of faith and to explain our findings. Success in this respect is, indeed, the leaven of liberty. No faith, no liberty!

Discords are as numerous as our forms of ignorance. Nearly all of mine are as unknown to me as yours to you. Why can this be said of everyone? Man, possessing but finite consciousness, has no more than infinitesimal glimpses of Infinite Consciousness—Creation. Therefore, the best anyone can do is to take note of the discords that fall within his limited awareness. Discords are countless, and I select two for comment, the first seemingly obvious, the second but a faint light in the darkness.

Ranking high in discord—out of harmony with freedom—are those who might be labeled *discontented socialists*. Not that they think of themselves as such—far from it! Indeed, these persons proclaim their horror of socialism, and they are as discontented with our present socialistic mess—inflation and despotism—as are our best freedom devotees.

Why label them socialists? Because their actions belie their words. It is one thing to preach freedom principles; it is quite another matter to practice them. These people by the millions talk against socialism, while at the same time they seek special privileges from federal, state or local governments—78,000 political pork barrels. Listing these errors is impossible. A generality must suffice: any request for governmental action that goes beyond keeping the peace and invoking a common justice falls in the socialistic category.

Now for the faint light in the darkness—a commentary on common discords seldom recognized. Admittedly, this speculation is way off in the far blue yonder.

Is it not an observed fact that the human species—over eons of time—has evolved, emerged, grown in awareness, perception, consciousness? Are not most people in our time ever so much more advanced in this respect than were cave dwellers, or the Cro-Magnons of 35 millennia ago? What accounts for this intellectual, moral and spiritual advance? We cannot penetrate this mystery, but we do see its effects. We can speculate, and while unable to prove my speculations, I fervently believe in them. They are founded on many personal experiences which, in my view, shed a bit of light on reality.

The reality as I see it? Infinite Consciousness—Creation—is a magnetic force attracting mankind toward the Infinite Order. Further, it appears to be a pulsating force like the tides, drawing and ceasing to draw in a sequence and on a vast range of frequencies.

Over and over again, and for many years, I have felt as if drawn by a magnet toward a spirit of inquiry—of wanting to know more. And in each instance, after a brief period, that attracting force, whatever it is, ceased, came to a dead halt—left me on my own, seemingly a test as to whether or not I had learned what the Divine Teacher had offered. If affirmative, inquiry progresses and the Teacher moves the student to a higher grade. More magnetism! If negative, inquiry is deadened!

Magnetic attraction fails to operate unless it finds a responsive substance. Sawdust, for instance, is not drawn to a magnet. Iron and steel filings are. Only things of a certain quality respond to magnetism.

Likewise, only those individuals who wish to learn respond to Creation's magnetism. Those who achieve this quality of openness continue to gain in consciousness. Countless individuals succeed more or less. Some keep going throughout their lives. Others soon quit when left on their own—their search at an end. Each failure is a discord; it is out of harmony with the Cosmic Plan and human destiny.

The author of that remarkable book, *Human Destiny,* wrote: "To really participate in the divine task, man must place his ideal as high as possible, out of reach if necessary."[1]

Faith in high ideals is, indeed, the leaven of liberty. To aim at liberty as an ideal is as high as one can go. Why? Liberty is the means, the key, to *human evolution!* Unless a person be free to act creatively as he pleases, he cannot participate in the Divine Task; he will be unable to achieve those other ideals—virtues—on which evolutionary upgrading depends.

Why, I wonder, have so many people lost faith in the efficacy of faith? Is it because they have a misplaced faith

---

[1]Lecomte du Noüy (New York: Longmans, Green & Co., 1947), p. 154.

in ignoble measures—despotism and the like—which are doomed to fail? The corrective? Attend to our aims in life; let the objectives be as high as possible, out of reach if necessary. Faith is an essential means to their attainment.

Finally, why did Robert Collyer claim that "Faith makes the discords of the present the harmonies of the future"? Answer the question, Why am I writing this piece? It is for precisely the same reason that many others are trying to think their way out of present evil into future good. The discords and errors that plague us stimulate the search for truths—harmonies of the future. What seem to be stumbling blocks in the countless forms of despotism are challenges; once they are faced and overcome they serve as steppingstones to liberty.

Wrote Archbishop Whately: "As the flower is before the fruit, so is faith before good works." *Have faith and we will win!*

3

HOPE

*The mighty hopes that make us
men.* **—TENNYSON**

During recorded history many wise men have expressed
their views of hope, and arrived at the most diverse conclusions. Victor Hugo, for instance, wrote, "Hope is a delu-
sion; no hand can grasp a wave or a shadow." Ever so many
others have given hope derogatory assessments. Why?
Hope may be based on unsound expectations, and thus the
mind of finite man, unless well-disciplined, has foolish
hopes galore.

On the other hand, there are many who glorify hope.
According to *I Corinthians* hope is one of the three heavenly
graces, the others being faith and charity. Hope, if foolish,
may be hellish, but if hope be wise, it is heavenly. A bit of
reflection on hope in its glorifying sense seems appropriate.
For what should we hope?

Hope, when viewed in the heavenly manner, is virtually a
prayer. Hoping that one may discover what is righteous is a

prayer not only for virtue but for an avoidance of error or wrongdoing. Tennyson spoke of "The mighty hopes that make us men." If our hopes be mighty in the heavenly sense, we shall be exemplary individuals.

Hope for an awareness of blessings—of all the foolish hopes, covetousness heads the list. It has been recognized as the origin of evil for centuries. The Tenth Commandment: "Thou shalt not covet." Covetousness leads to actions that range all the way from theft to our present welfare state—the something-for-nothing syndrome.

While it's possible for governmental laws to penalize living off others, such laws cannot do away with the desire. Bear in mind that covetousness has as many variations as there are individuals who covet.

The overcoming of this foolish hope is a personal problem. The remedy? An awareness of one's blessings. Each of us has more than he can count. Every misery one misses is a blessing, as is every breath of fresh air, every friend, every enlightening thought. Covetousness cannot abide in the soul of anyone who is aware of his countless blessings.

Hope for youth—"One does not grow old. One becomes old by not growing."

Most people associate youth with childhood and adolescence. But youth is a certain spirit and temper and not necessarily just the early time of one's life. Once adulthood is reached, youth is assumed to be in the past tense. Such an outlook dismisses growth as a potentiality of human beings. Acorns grow into tall oaks and we can grow every year of our lives.

An enlightening book of the 1930's was *Life Begins at Forty,* by Walter Pitkin. The author could as well have said fifty or even eighty! Indeed, life should make new beginnings during every moment of our mortal existence. The Greek philosopher, Heraclitus, wrote, "Man is on earth as in an egg." This inspired C. S. Lewis to remark, "Now, you cannot go on being a good egg forever; you must either hatch or rot."

The explanation as to why so many rot on the vine, as we say—life's mission at an end—is that they fail to recognize an undeniable truth expressed by the eminent psychologist, Fritz Kunkel: "*Immense hidden powers* lurk in the unconscious of the most common man—indeed, of all people without exception."

Hoping for youth—growing day-in-and-day-out—eliminates the need of hoping for the joyful life or intelligence or the diminution of faults. These blessings are the dividends of perpetual youth—of never growing old!

Hope for a sense of justice—Justice is "the quality of being righteous; impartiality; fairness." It is truth—as nearly as one can discern it—in daily practice.

Those of us interested in a return to the freedom way of life should keep Burke's wisdom in mind, "Whenever a separation is made between liberty and justice, neither, in my opinion, is safe." Our hope—prayer—for a personal sense of justice will bring no endowments unless we know and observe at least two simple behavioral rules:

- Do not unto others that which you would not have them do unto you.

- Apply the principle of universality to one's maxims or beliefs. Briefly, never do anything which would bring on chaos if everyone did the same. By the same token, act creatively as you please and concede to all others that identical privilege.

Here, in a nutshell, is John Stuart Mill's formula for the daily practice of justice:

The only freedom which deserves the name, is that of pursuing our own good in our own way, so long as we do not attempt to deprive others of theirs, or impede their efforts to obtain it.

When government is limited to its proper function, law is justice!

Hope for humility—There are numerous virtues and vices that account for the rise and fall of societies. Near the top of the list are the two opposites, humility and pride. Let's take a look at the latter, beginning with a piece of ancient wisdom from Proverbs 14:18: "Pride goeth before destruction, and a haughty spirit before a fall."

Pride sprouts and grows from ignorance and self-blindness. Those with a haughty spirit foolishly believe they know the most, whereas they know the least. While they don't know how to make a pencil or why grass is green or who we are, they "know" how to run our lives. In their blind pride, the least taste of political power drives them to become power addicts. Until such persons seek help, there is little we can do to curb their addiction. What we can and must do is to develop in ourselves the strength of character to resist the temptations of power.

The strength of character each of us should develop is true humility—the state of being teachable in mind and spirit. Humility is an awareness of how much there is to learn; it is a virtue that displaces the sin of pride. No person can be a know-it-all at the same time that he seriously seeks knowledge.

Humility is to make a right estimate of self and this Socrates did, saying, "I know that I know nothing but I know I know nothing." Reflection reveals the fact that the more one knows the more he knows he does not know. As Saint Augustine phrased it, "The sufficiency of my merit is to know that my merit is not sufficient."

"Humility, like darkness, reveals the heavenly lights." Grasping the sinfulness of pride reveals the heavenly virtue of humility—the only remedy for ridding society of power addicts.

Hail to the humble!

Hope for integrity—Wrote Emerson, "I cannot find language of sufficient energy to convey my sense of *the sacredness of integrity.*" For a man of Emerson's genius in thinking and phrasing, this is quite a confession. Indeed, so much neglected is this virtue that Bernard Dougall's assessment applies to most individuals, "Integrity was a word he couldn't even spell, let alone define."

The definition as I phrase it: Integrity is the accurate reflection in word and deed of what one believes to be righteous—no deviations, none whatsoever. Absolute consistency! Lacking a leadership to set such a standard, the freedom way of life is impossible.

An example of the required leadership is found in Matthew 4:22:

The light of the body is the eye; if therefore thine eye be single, thy whole body shall be full of light.

How is this to be phrased in understandable terms? Obviously, the "light of the body" refers to enlightenment. The "eye," of course, is perception—seeing.

"If the eye be single!" what possibly can this mean? Refer to Webster for a definition of "single" as here used: "Not deceitful or artful, simple, honest, sincere." Wrote Shakespeare, "I speak with a *single* heart."

Single in this sense is directly linked with *integer,* meaning "whole, entire, not divided." Thus, *single* refers to that blessed virtue, *integrity*.

Contrasted to single is double which has the same original root as "duplicity." Such phrasings as "double dealing" and "double talk" convey this connotation—that damnable vice.

Phrased in modern American idiom, Matthew's insight would read:

Enlightenment of the intellect and spirit of man depends on his powers of perception, and if these powers be free from duplicity, that is, if they be grounded in pure integrity, man will be as much graced with enlightenment—wisdom—as is within his capability.

For freedom's sake let us aspire to be so graced!

4

CHARITY

*A man should fear only the good
he does publicly.*
—HENRY WARD BEECHER

St. Paul wrote the following words in his letter to the church in Corinth:

> And now abideth faith, hope, charity, these three: but the greatest of these is charity.

My fervent wish to understand Paul's assertion inspires the following speculations.

Some things are obvious if one gives serious thought to this subject. For instance, there may be no greater menace to society, here or elsewhere, than government handouts—misconceived as charity. Implicit in the operations of socialism—the welfare state—is helping people to become helpless. The state does this by giving out food stamps, paying farmers not to farm, workers not to work, and so on. This policy deadens self-responsibility, the very essence of one's being.

Why this misfortune? Why do millions of socialistically oriented people fall into this politico-economic trap? They fail to recognize that their give-aways consist of goods and services forcibly withdrawn from the free market which produced them—that much maligned and handicapped free market which their schemes have not yet destroyed. And they "think" of this as charity! It is the very opposite! This kind of "good"—all done publicly and for publicity's sake—should, indeed be feared.

In writing of "Charity: Biblical and Political," The Reverend Russell J. Clinchy has stressed the point:

> If we need laws to make people treat men of other faiths and races as friends; if we need the police power of the secular state to take money from men for human need; if it is believed that the only hope of a city of God is to seek the alternative of a collectivized mass leveled to the lowest common denominator of mentality and ability—if all this be the limit of our hope for mankind, then even such activity is sheer futility, for even if such an effort could be achieved it would have no meaning at all for mankind. This rejection of personal responsibility would prove only that it is possible to make men live like whipped dogs, and the proving of it would be hell.

It is largely forgotten, unfortunately, that true charity is a highly spiritual attainment. Here it is as written in Matthew 6:

> When you do some act of charity, *do not let your left hand know what your right hand is doing: your good deed must be in secret,* and your Father who sees what is done in secret, will reward you.

According to this scriptural passage, not only must the recipient of one's kindness be unaware of the identity of the giver but charity in this spiritual sense requires also that the giver immediately erase from his mind any record of what he gave with joy and love. The deed is done, forget it.

In a sense, to hear of someone's urgent need for help is like listening to his private prayer. To respond charitably to that person's prayer is never undertaken as an obligation to him but as a cleansing of one's own conscience. If one responds, he does so for his own sake and the pure joy of doing it. And that closes the book, balances that particular account. The sooner the giver can forget it, the more receptive he may be to other opportunities to develop and use his God-given faculties. "Every good wish is a prayer and every good deed is an answer to a prayer."

Whenever one rises to this spiritual height, secrecy to self as well as to others becomes a built-in trait, as natural and no more reflected upon than breathing or heart beats. This is true charity—and the rewards are out of this world![1]

------

[1] A remarkable book on this subject is *Magnificent Obsession* by Lloyd C. Douglas (New York, 1969).

5

LET THE OBJECTIVE
BE HIGH

*High aims form high characters,
and great objects bring out great
minds.* **—TRYON EDWARDS**

Millions of our countrymen—young and elderly, male and female—have intellectual, moral and spiritual potentialities that are never realized. Minds which could be great do not rise above their aims and objectives. If the string be short, no kite will fly high. And if life's objectives be low, no high character will be formed.

There is no such thing as a mass objective or a mass error. There are only individual aims and actions which tend toward a dull sameness. Before highlighting a great objective that brings out great minds, here is a sampling of our behaviors that stifle human progress.

- A citizen built a nice home on a 2-acre lot which had no trees. He took several saplings from a *public* park

21

across the road rather than pay for them at a *private* nursery. Theft!

In precisely the same category are the actions of those millions of Americans who employ the coercive force of government to feather their own nests at the expense of others. This is to legalize thievery, and there is no difference *in principle* between legal and illegal theft. No high characters are ever formed when dragged down by such low aims.

- Examine a wide spectrum of human behaviors and, in more cases than not, personal advantage is sought through expediency, and lying is its accomplice. Lies are the means to ignoble objectives, about as low as one can aim. Wrote Oliver Wendell Holmes: "Sin has many tools, but a lie is the handle which fits them all." The fear of telling the truth as one sees the truth is the genesis of most fibbing.

Such dubious notions as the following cause a great deal of low-grade behavior:

- To tell the truth as I see it would make me look like a fool.
- I can gain the favor of others by saying what I think they would like to hear from me.
- I shall never lie except to shield myself.
- Really, there is no harm in telling a white lie.

The result? "This is the punishment of a liar. He is not believed even when he tells the truth." "Liars begin by imposing upon others, but end by deceiving themselves." To thus abuse one's talent and waste one's potential dooms life to mediocrity! Great minds are not brought out by this sin.

- Ever so many people have no higher objective than notoriety, applause, fame; in which case the eye is cast, not at the stars, but at popularity. Such people are depressed when failing and fatheaded when succeeding. No great minds from those so motivated!
- Reflect upon the many who think of riches as the only end in life. It follows that they are blind to all higher goals. They are bogged down at the King Midas level.
- Civilizations rise as slavery fades away and fall as slavery increases. Slavery? It is measured by the extent to which effort is *compulsorily* expended for the "benefit" of others instead of self-benefit, as happens when government takes from some in order to subsidize others.

The countless authors of slavery—those who resort to coercion—are in all walks of life. Among our Simon Legrees are those who falsify by claiming agreement with majority opinion in order to gain political power. So are those who sponsor legislation to prohibit free entry and competition, be they labor or business "leaders." Advocacy of the planned society, be it from pulpits or classrooms, gives birth to slavery.

Let me now highlight a great objective, one that brings out great minds—the greatest politico-economic phenomenon ever conceived by the mind of man. It is the private property, free market, limited government way of life. In this, as distinguished from its opposite—socialism—there is no dulling sameness. The devotees of freedom are few and far between, a fact which, if understood, is not at all discouraging.

As Emerson wrote, "The end pre-exists in the means."

Evil behavior must always lead to an evil way of life precisely as righteous ways lead to the good life. Here is a thought we can add to Emerson's: High ends pre-exist in high methods. Aiming high results in ends that gratify! Note the distinctions between the low and the high ways.

The positive counterpart of stealing is to so use your own property that others will respect your ownership; and to defend to the best of your own abilities and resources every other person's rightful claim to property.

- These rare individuals would never steal a loaf of bread even if they or their families were in a state of hunger. Nor would they ever, under any circumstances, approve of government doing the robbing for them. To the contrary, they would cast their voices and votes against such political chicanery, not by denunciation but by explaining the virtues of honesty. "Thou shalt not steal."

The positive counterpart of lying is to know the truth and so live it that it shines through to effectively light the way for others.

- Lying? They would tell the truth as they see it even if everyone were to disagree. They seek their approval before God [righteousness], not men. "The truth shall make you free."

The positive counterpart of the urge for popular acclaim—vanity—is the humble and inquiring mind.

- Popularity? They couldn't care less! As with lying, they seek only righteousness, the aim that brings out great minds.

The positive counterpart of the love of riches is the constructive use of one's talents.

- Wealth has but a single purpose: freeing individuals from the mundane chores in order that they may discover and develop their unique capabilities.

The positive counterpart of slavery is personal freedom of choice in the development and use of one's abilities in the human form of private ownership and free trade.

- These few devotees of freedom would permit everyone to act *creatively* as he or she pleases, produce whatever goods or services they choose and freely exchange with anyone in this or other countries. As to the social agency—government—they would limit it to the protection of ownership—anti-slavery—and to invoking a common justice by inhibiting all destructive actions.

In summary, the star of freedom is surely one of life's highest objectives. And the steps along the way should be in harmony with that high goal. Lesser means can only lead to baser ends—never toward freedom. Thus, let the objectives be high, that we may realize our potentialities.

6

REFLECTIONS ON HOPE AND FEAR

Hope is like the sun, which, as we journey toward it, casts the shadow of our burden behind us.
—SAMUEL SMILES

Hopes and fears, from the sublime to the ridiculous, beset all of us all of our lives. Such aspirations and dejections might envision periods of time ranging from the momentary to the eternal. But our concern here is with the hopes and fears of freedom devotees in our times. And let us begin with the hopeful.

Hope is one of the mainsprings of human progress. It can, indeed, be likened to the sun. As our hopes for liberty are strengthened—as we journey toward their realization—our burden, the authoritarian shadow, is cast behind us. Hope for the ideal leads to intellectual enlightenment, and darkness has no resistance to this light!

Hope has several essential elements, three of which are here examined:

26

• *Expectation*—This is born of wanting to know more and to have more—materially and/or intellectually. There is no stage in human progress—ancient or modern—when expectation should subside. Indeed, the more we progress the more should this yearning for learning stimulate our actions.

The president of a leading auto firm remarked to me in 1954, "The problem of production has been solved." No expectation of the autos to come! Actually, the problem of production was no more solved in 1954 than today—or prior to the invention of the wheel! To conclude otherwise is to declare expectation at an end—hope deadened.

Expectation includes items not possessed but hoped for. Example: there would not be even one pencil had not the value of pencils been envisioned. Hope for the what-is-not is the genesis of the what-is and of the what-will-be!

• *Confidence*—Progress is attained by those who have confidence in winning. From the English poet, Alexander Pope, we learn that:

> By mutual confidence and mutual aid
> Great deeds are done, and great dis-
> coveries made.

Mutual confidence and mutual aid are basic features of the freedom to own, to produce, and to exchange: the source of great discoveries.

• *Faith*—What more need be said of the importance of faith than is told us in these lines:

All the strength and force of man comes from *the faith in things unseen*. He who believes is strong; he who doubts is weak. Strong convictions precede great actions.

Have faith!

As asserted in Proverbs 29:18, "Where there is no vision, the people perish." And, assuredly, the people would perish were there no hope among those of us who love liberty. In the absence of hope the free society could not exist. Why? Those who know not how to run their own lives would program ours, reducing the people to *programmed robots*. If such a low status be not a living death—as related to life's high purpose—pray tell, what is!

Now to some reflections on fear. Wrote the author and editor, C. N. Bovee:

There is great beauty in going through life without anxiety or fear. Half our fears are baseless and the other half discreditable.

As with hope, fear has several essential elements, three of which are here examined:

● *Timidity*—"Woe unto timid hearts and faint hands."

When men are timid, they no longer stand upright or dare each to speak what is in his own mind. Progress is not spawned by such beings. The U.S.A. is presently facing a crisis, one reason being that millions in all walks of life fear censure or loss of face or votes or business. Wrote Plautus, "A man that's timid in a crisis isn't worth a penny."

● *Suspicion*—Suspicious individuals—those who always

suspect others' motives—breed suspicion in return. This casts the eye away from what's right, and searching for the right is the only remedy for imbecility.

Suspicion is no less an enemy to virtue than to happiness. He that is already corrupt is naturally suspicious, and he that becomes suspicious will quickly become corrupt. —*Samuel Johnson*

Suspicion is far more apt to be wrong than right; oftener unjust than just. It is no friend to virtue, and always an enemy to happiness. —*Hosea Ballou*

• *Cowardice*—To know what is right and take a conflicting position is cowardice at its worst. This evil is rooted in the fallacy that it is dangerous to be honest. The fact? It is destructive of self and others *not* to live a life of integrity. Fear is a hellish trait!

Socrates spoke of himself as a philosophical midwife. I would humbly aspire to a similar function, receiving from ever so many sources, and then sharing the findings with anyone interested.

Ralph Bradford, in his autobiography, *One Man's Life,* tells how he received a brilliant idea about the meaning of direction from Dorothy Pillsbury. He relates that in her charming book, *No High Abode,* she tells of mentioning the four cardinal compass points to her Mexican neighbor, Mrs. Apodaca, and the latter replied: "Did you know, Señora, that Los Indios have two more directions? Not only do they have North, East, South and West, but they have Up and Down. And I," she added, "have still another one. It is El Centro—the Center. It is good to know in what direction

you go . . . but it is *muy importante*—very important—to
know where you stand right now. That is the Center."

And then Bradford elaborates the theme in three paragraphs that I would like to share with you as follows: "East
and West; North and South; Up and Down; In and Out;
Center—the place where we are. In these phrases I have
reached for symbols that might help us orient ourselves in
the vast dimension of time. And I come back, finally, to Up,
which is both actually and metaphorically the most significant direction of all.

"When we express man's growth and progress we think
always of rising from lower to higher levels—Up—beyond
turbo-jets and rockets; Up—to the inconceivable vastness
of space, where the great stars blaze and die and are born
again in the endless process of creation.

"Up, finally, to a spiritual height that transcends all else,
*to a vista compounded of hope and faith and desperate soul
hunger.* In this bewildering age of the atom, when our quest
for knowledge brings us to the verge of self-destruction, and
there is a chilling fear deep in every life; when we are
bewildered by the cynical overturning of ancient altars and
old moralities—in such a time it is comforting to reach
beyond the torments and confusions that come of our
knowledge, and lean with a sense of security upon the arm
of faith."

Down with fear! Up with Faith and Hope that life's high
purpose may be increasingly approached!

7

SEEKING SAVES SOULS

Ask, and it shall be given you;
seek, and ye shall find; knock,
and it shall be opened unto you.
For every one that asketh re-
ceives; and he that seeketh find-
eth; and to him that knocketh
it shall be opened.

—MATTHEW 7:7-8

We don't talk much about the soul these days, and if you are more comfortable with words like mind, or psyche, or consciousness that's all right with me. I refer to "an entity which is regarded as being the immortal or the spiritual part of the person." Briefly, the soul is separate and apart from the physical and relates only to *consciousness,* that phase of the individual which is immortalized—eternal and forever. It is only by persistent seeking that we may discover and save this elusive part of our total make-up.

The extent to which we grow in consciousness measures the extent to which we rise above the animal, or go beyond the physical. Thus, achievement in this respect is life's highest purpose—ascending as far as possible from the mere mortal to the immortal. Those seeking how to so live—

31

looking for the magic key—might well abide by an ancient wisdom: *"he that seeketh findeth!"*

The above verse from Matthew does not mean that all shall be readily opened unto us—that Infinite Consciousness will be our reward, within our reach. Instead, it means that seeking opens the way to an increasing consciousness, and the more elevated and proficient the seeking, the more will be opened unto us.

Wrote William Hazlitt, "When a thing ceases to be a subject of controversy it ceases to be a subject of interest." This thesis of mine ought to be of interest for it exhibits a high potential disagreement! There are, on the one hand, countless atheists and, on the other, such oversouls— spiritual transcendentalists—as Ralph Waldo Emerson, the Sage of Concord.

An atheist is one who believes that there is nothing in Creation beyond his and other finite minds. Immortality is nonsense, there being nothing beyond one's mortal or earthly moments. Thus, so far as this subject is concerned, an atheist is god—there is no God! Numerous atheists of my acquaintance are famous or wealthy or both—life's mission achieved! Should I condemn these atheistically oriented folks? No, for I believe in freedom of choice or, as that oversoul, Elbert Hubbard, expressed it, "Do unto others as if you were the others."

The very opposite of atheism is transcendentalism:

. . . any of various philosophies that propose to discover the nature of reality by investigating the process of thought rather than the objects of sense experience . . . based on a search for reality through *spiritual intuition*.

There have been and are many individuals graced with spiritual intuition—cognitive flashes ranging from a few to thousands. The root of this blessing? Seeking!

The question before all other questions concerns priorities. What seek ye first? It is an admonishment appearing in Matthew 6:33:

> But seek ye first the Kingdom of God and his Righteousness [Truth] and all these things [material well-being] shall be added unto you.

Paraphrasing C. S. Lewis:

> Aim at Heaven [Truth] and we will get earth [wealth] thrown in. Aim at earth and we will get neither.

True, there are those who aim only at fame and fortune [earth] and succeed. But it is only because there are those—past and present—who aim at Heaven [Truth]. Were all to aim at earth, there would be no enlightenment and, thus, no wealth. Fame? So what! Hitler achieved that!

Enlightenment should be our ambition during every mortal moment. "To kill time is to damage eternity." Seeking—day in and day out—is the key to ascendancy. And the road to seeking is paved with prayer. But not prayer by rote—"by memory alone, without understanding or thought." *Meaningless!* Emerson enlightens us:

> Is not prayer a study of truth, a sally of the soul into the *unfound infinite?* . . . No man ever prayed heartily without learning something.

Heartily? It means with zest, enthusiasm or, better yet, from the heart! *Meaningful!*

Several thoughts on meaningful prayer, the kind that enlightens the self and, thus, becomes a partial answer in itself:

- May my daily behaviors manifest charity, intelligence, justice, humility, love, integrity, and reverence for life.
- May I learn to recognize more and more of my blessings, for they are countless!
- I pray for Thy blessings upon our associates—oversouls—near and far, past and present, the perfection of our ideas and ideals, our adherence to them, our efforts, our judgments, our faith in Thee.
- May I make progress in overcoming those countless faults of mine which stand as obstacles to those of Thy ways which might possibly be manifested through me.
- I pray for an increasingly sensitive ability to harmonize my actions and thoughts with Thy Divine and Infinite wisdom and love that I may more nearly do Thy Will.
- May I develop those qualities that will be attracted to Thy Infinite Wisdom.

While certain that seeking is a soul-saving procedure, I do not know and perhaps no individual has ever known all the self-disciplines for perfect seeking. To grasp how devoted seeking works its wonders is comparable in difficulty to understanding and explaining with clarity how freedom works its wonders. Both border on the celestial. Each is a star in the far, blue yonder.

Aim at the sun and you may not reach it; but your arrow will fly far higher than if aimed at an object on a level with yourself.   —*Joel Hawkes*

Aiming at the sun—Truth and Righteousness—requires

another discipline, second only to prayer. It is to record in writing all ideas and insights the moment they flash into mind. Why? Ideas are as effervescent as dreams. Unless recorded at once they are gone forever. Try never to lose a single one of these precious blessings—building blocks to potential, personal knowledge.

Will Durant gives this thesis an appropriate conclusion:

Knowledge is the eye of desire and can become the pilot of the soul!

8

CHARACTER

Institutions and laws are but the outward manifestations or outcome of the underlying ideas, sentiments, customs, in short, character. To urge a different outcome would in no way alter men's character—or the outcome.
—GUSTAV LE BON

Why do I rate the above by this French psychologist and sociologist (1841-1931) as a penetrating insight? A confession: I completely agree with it! Those who disagree—and most would—may call it foolishness; but our differing opinions are subjective judgments.

As to agreement: I have repeated over the years, long before reading this author, that whatever shows forth on the political horizon is no more than an echoing or reflection of whatever the preponderant thinking happens to be at any given time. Complete agreement—different phrasing, that's all.

Were I to descend from outer space, with these convictions in mind, and had a look at the kind of governments we now have, I would conclude that the preponderant thinking is anti-freedom—authoritarian. And, further, that there is no chance for betterment except as the underlying ideas, sentiments and customs are modified to favor freedom.

It follows that an ascending or descending society is nothing more nor less than a response to good or bad thinking. An ancient wisdom: "As he thinketh in his heart so is he." (Proverbs 23:7) The best society that ever existed was the result of superb thinking on the part of our Founding Fathers. The decline into socialism which we are now experiencing is due to bad thinking by ever so many of our contemporaries.

It is thinking, and thinking only, that divides right from wrong; it is thinking and thinking only that elevates or degrades societies. What we "think in the heart" governs the future: elevation or degradation. That remarkable genius in music, theology, poetry, medicine and philosophy, Albert Schweitzer, wrote:

> Living truth is that alone which has its origin in thinking. Just as a tree bears year after year the same fruit and yet fruit which is each year new, so must *all permanently valuable ideas be continually born again in thought.*

While Schweitzer may not have had the U.S.A.'s present dilemma in mind, this is assuredly sage counsel for all of us. In what respect? *Those sanctified ideas and ideals of our Founding Fathers must be born again!*

Let us analyze the old proverb, "As he thinketh in his heart so is he," and ask what is meant by heart? Assuredly, the reference is not to the muscular organ of that name. Rather, what we have here is a metaphor—a figure of speech for one's true nature—"*inmost* thoughts and feelings; consciousness or conscience." This is virtually synonymous with *character:* "a distinctive trait or attribute; essential quality; nature . . . moral constitution."

A seemingly correct conclusion is that a man's *thinking* is rooted in his *character*. Individual character determines not only what one thinks, but also what he makes of his life. Our ambition for a recovery of freedom in America depends on more persons with character coming to the fore by power of example. For enlightenment, I seek and herewith share some thoughts on character by men of character.

- Talents are best nurtured in solitude; character is best formed in the stormy billows of the world.   —*Goethe*

- A man's character is the reality of himself. His reputation is the opinion others have formed of him. Character is in him; reputation is from other people. Character is the substance, reputation is the shadow.
                                                    —*Henry Ward Beecher*

- Our character is but the stamp on our souls of the free choices of good and evil we have made through life.
                                                    —*Cunningham Geikie*

- We want the spirit of America to be efficient; we want American character to be efficient; we want American character to display itself in what I may, perhaps, be allowed to call spiritual efficiency—clear disinterested thinking and fearless action along the right lines of thought.   —*Woodrow Wilson*

- Not education, but character, is man's greatest need and man's greatest safeguard.   —*Herbert Spencer*

- It is not money, nor is it mere intellect that governs the world; it is moral character, and intellect associated with moral excellence.   —*T. D. Woolsey*

- Character, that sublime health which values one moment as another. *—Emerson*

- 'Tis character persuades, not empty words. *—Plutarch*

- Man's character is his fate. *—Heraclitus*

- A good character carries with it the highest power of causing a thing to be believed. *—Aristotle*

- It is not the brains that matter most, but that which guides them—the character, the heart, generous qualities, progressive ideas. *—Fydor Dostoyevski*

- The noblest contribution which any man can make for the benefit of posterity, is that of a good character. The richest bequest which any man can leave to the youth of his native land, is that of a shining, spotless example. *—R. C. Winthrop*

- Good character is human nature in its best form. It is moral order embodied in the individual. Men of character are not only the conscience of society, but in every well governed state they are its best motive power; for it is moral qualities which, in the main rule the world. *—Samuel Smiles*

If the U.S.A. is again to become an orderly, freedom-oriented nation, only men of character—as were our Founding Fathers—can perform the miracle. The mere urging of character or outcome is utterly futile, as Le Bon observed; it is to spin our wheels, as the saying goes.

What, then, should be your and my ambition? Become a person of character—*a shining, spotless example*!

9

COURAGE

To see what is right and not do it,
is want of courage.

—CONFUCIUS

My shoe manufacturing friend seems to side with Confucius: "I am the only one in this business who refused to sign a petition that would outlaw foreign imports of shoes." No want of courage there!

Numerous wise men—past and present—have emphasized this point. Wrote Cicero, "Courage is that virtue which champions the cause of right." And Mark Twain adds, "Always do right. *This will gratify some people and startle the rest."*

In view of the fact that no two persons think exactly alike, how shall we interpret Twain's advice, "Always do right"? No individual knows all the truth and nothing but the truth. Thus, no two persons will have identical answers to this question. Here is my understanding of what is right: The accurate reflection in word and deed of whatever one's highest consciousness dictates as righteous. There is only one great adventure, and that is directed inward—self-improvement.

Those whose lives are featured by the great adventure are not only *gratified* but blest by the very few others who are thus ascending. And those among the countless millions who pay no heed to courage, as here defined, are *startled!* Why this bewilderment? They regard it as dangerous to be honest—to do right as one sees the right!

History presents several examples of the "dangers" that follow doing right as one sees the right. The outstanding example comes to mind of Jesus on the cross. Yet, when viewed aright, His life and tragic end conferred upon mankind a blessing of the highest order. The lesson? The fear of danger may block the way to Eternal Truth. That honesty is the best policy is affirmed by Alexander Pope: "An honest man's the noblest work of God."

The courage to do the right as one sees the right came to me as a personal enlightenment over 30 years ago. I was invited to an evening session with a dozen of America's leading businessmen, met to devise ways of resisting government encroachments. I was shocked at their evasiveness; they wanted to hire someone to fight their battles. "We'll handsomely pay some professor to present our views to the Senate Committee." When they finally asked for my view, I feared the danger in voicing my strong dissent—they'll hate me. Then the behavior of my great mentor, W. C. Mullendore, flashed into mind. What would Bill say? "Tell them the truth as you see it." So I explained that this was not an errand to be farmed out but a personal responsibility of first magnitude, demanding their personal involvement and commitment. Yes, all but two were shocked. However, from then on, all of these men respected and sought my views. Why? Because I had overcome my fear of being honest!

Here is a current experience. One of our country's most

patriotic and spiritual journals has, for the past several years, reprinted numerous essays of mine. And what a favorable response from some of its distinguished readers—excited about the freedom philosophy.

The brilliant publisher of this journal was shocked by a recent essay of mine—"Why Not Separate School and State?" He favored government education. Result? That journal is now featuring socialistic education. Bad? No, it is all to the good!

Why is the action of my publisher friend all to the good? He has the courage to do the right as he sees the right. True, what he sees as right—government education—is at odds with what I see as right—free market education. We differ in what we see but we both appreciate the merit of courage. Had more of us than now the courage to do the right— regardless of differences—economic, intellectual, moral and spiritual ascendancy would grace our way of life. In the absence of courage, falsehood dominates society. Shakespeare gave us an everlasting guideline:

> To thine own self be true,
> And it must follow, as the night the day,
> Thou canst not then be false to any man.

If one's ambition be to advance the freedom way of life, his first step is to decide what society's agency of organized force—government—should and should not do. How draw the line? My answer: Limit government to invoking a common justice, keeping the peace and inhibiting all destructive actions such as fraud, violence and the like. *Leave all constructive activities—no exceptions—*to men acting creatively as they please!

If there be any activity that falls in the creative realm, education most certainly belongs there. Coercion is antagonistic to learning. Point 10 in the *Communist Manifesto* reads, "Free education for all children in public schools." Public, that is, government, education in the U.S.A. is not only not "free," it has three forms of coercion: (1) compulsory attendance, (2) government dictated curricula and (3) the forcible collection of the wherewithal to pay the bills. Leave education to the free and unfettered market where the wisdom is!

Why do so many feel a reverence for government education? Because it's part of our mores! Wrap the American flag around any socialistic activity and shortly a vast majority will regard it as Americanism—the postal "system" is an example. Whenever government pre-empts any activity, all thinking about alternate free-market procedure is deadened—settled into the ruts of custom. Government education falls in this category, mistakenly adopted nearly two centuries ago: Americanism!

Finally, reflect on the potential talents that are lost to human welfare for the want of courage to do the right as one sees the right. Assuming courage on both sides, the failure of another to see what I see or vice versa is no longer the issue. Instead, a rewarding tactic comes within our view— sharing with each other what we see, the formula for improving conscience and enlightenment. "To see what is right and not do it is a want of courage."

Let us do it!

10

ORDER

Order is light, peace, inward liberty, free command over oneself; it is power. . . . It is aesthetic and moral beauty; it is well-being; it is man's greatest need. **—AMIEL**

Henri Frederic Amiel (1821-81), that remarkable Swiss philospher who devoted a lifetime to his private journal— "written for my own consolation and warning." Several generations of readers have been inspired by the thoughts of this intensive thinker, and it was back in 1951 that I was first introduced to these pages. One of the first of Amiel's thoughts to hit home was this: "A man only understands that of which he has already the beginnings in himself."[1] Briefly, if one is to grasp the wisdom of the ages—past and present—he must strive for beginnings in his own mind, on and on, endlessly!

So let us begin with order, that "free command over oneself" looked upon by Amiel as "man's greatest need." Assuredly, if one does not order his own life, he will be ordered about by others.

Order is not a simple concept; as Amiel understands it,

---

[1] An entry of December 17, 1854 in *Journal Intime* of Henri Amiel.

order has many facets. It might be instructive to discuss the several features, as he lists them.

Order is light. In John 12:46 we find the words, "I am come a light into the world." The metaphor here clearly suggests *Enlightenment!*

Pursue this analogy further: It is easily demonstrable that darkness offers no resistance and readily gives way to light. It should also be clear that ignorance is powerless against enlightenment, though the process of learning seems slow and uncertain at best and many despair that it can occur at all within a given society. Why such skepticism? Is it not because the enlightenment of even the best of us is so dim relative to Infinite Enlightenment that we observe little advancement of others by reason of what we have to share?

To grasp this point, look not into the dark—our effect on the improvement of others. Rather, observe how each of us has taken little steps away from ignorance toward enlightenment by reason of numerous individuals—Amiel, for instance.

Yes, order is light. And Amiel's point is that orderliness in the mind of the individual is the key to his own enlightenment and to the light which he in turn may offer to others.

Order is peace. As Bastiat wrote, "When goods do not cross borders soldiers will." Free traders are the ambassadors of peace and good will—the ambassadors of righteousness. It is right that everyone should be free to act creatively as he pleases, and this includes exchanging goods and services with anyone who is willing and able, either at home or abroad. The Biblical pronouncement sets neither geographic nor political boundaries. "Glory to God in the highest, and on earth peace, *good will* toward men." (Luke

2:14) As testimony, observe the peaceful relationships between those in our 50 states—the world's largest free-trade area.

The dictionary defines order as "a state of peace and serenity . . . orderly conduct." That's the harmonious state of mankind when freedom prevails.

Order is inward liberty. Liberty is, indeed, an inward accomplishment. You can no more bestow liberty on me or I on you than either of us can bestow intelligence, integrity, humility or any virtue on each other. Liberty does not descend on us but, rather, it is a blessing to which each ascends. Liberty must be earned to be enjoyed. We bring order and joy to our lives by this inward ascension!

Order is a free command over oneself. For an example of "a free command over oneself," observe those few people who adhere strictly to the old maxim, "A place for everything and everything in its place"—be it in the kitchen, living room, garden or wherever. They have an aversion to sloppiness—disorder—and want nothing to do with things or actions in disarray.

These individuals adhere to their orderly formula in numerous ways. For instance, punctuality is a habit—on time for all engagements—and they keep their promises. Sloppiness—a place for nothing and nothing in its place—is taboo. Give us a few more people like this and the ordering of our lives by politicians and bureaucrats would also be taboo!

Order is power. Those who live their lives aright *never* exert power over another's life or even think of doing so. Rather, all the power they possess is directed toward an improvement of their own thoughts, ideas and ideals. This is a *moral* power! An American clergyman, Horace Bushnell (1802-76), added his wisdom on this important phase of life:

> By moral power we mean the power of a life and a character, the power of good and great purposes, the power which comes at length to reside in a man distinguished in some course of estimable or great conduct. . . . No other power of man compares with this, and *there is no individual who may not be measurably invested with it.*

Order is aesthetic and moral beauty.   Most people think of order *only* as an orderly desk or workshop or restaurant or attire—a commendable neatness in all personal matters. Order to them means stable, unchanging situations in every aspect of life, be it social or personal. As a consequence, they are led into a fallacy; stabilize the social situation!

The first step, if we would remedy this fallacy, is to realize that no two among our some 200 million citizens are remotely alike in talents or expertise or potentialities. Further, no individual today is identical to the self he was yesterday. Everything in the Cosmos, be it atoms or galaxies or man, is in constant change. Any attempt to stabilize the what-is, as related to social affairs, is an affront to evolution—Creation at whatever level!

What, then, is order as related to the politico-economic—social—situation? It is the freedom to take advantage of this constant flux. Let all the trillions times trillions of tiny creativities freely flow and configurate, so that creation at the human level may be more and more realized. These flowing, ever-changing activities—not stabilization—compose the order for which we should strive. *This is moral beauty!* Wrote the historian, George Bancroft (1801-81):

Beauty is but the sensible image of the Infinite. . . . Like truth and justice it lives within us; like virtue and the moral law it is a companion of the soul.

Order is well-being. Says the dictionary, "Virtue is essential to the well-being of man." Thus, according to Amiel, order—well-being—has its wellspring or fountainhead in virtues. Goethe observed that "All truly wise ideas have been thought already thousands of times." An excellent example of this truth is the following by an English clergyman, Caleb C. Colton (1780-1832), written several decades before Amiel:

There is but one pursuit in life which is in the power of all to follow, and of all to attain. It is subject to no disappointments since he that perseveres makes every difficulty an advancement, and every conquest a victory; and this is the pursuit of virtue. Sincerely to aspire after virtue is to gain her; and zealously to labor after her ways is to receive them.

Order is man's greatest need. Admittedly, Amiel's observations as stated at the beginning are highly esoteric and, as written, can rarely be understood. Doubtless, some of the wisest thoughts of man over the ages have never been grasped.

Why dwell on or try to unravel Amiel's thoughts as related to order? He was a wise man! By quoting other sages—bringing them to our aid—I have, if only for myself, tried to gain some enlightenment.

If there be some accuracy in these deductions, then order is, indeed, among man's greatest needs. Accept order as revealed by this great thinker and we have a solid foundation for human liberty.

11

THE CAPTAIN IS ON
THE BRIDGE

*Great peace have they which love
thy law; and nothing shall offend
them.* **—PSALMS 119:165**

For the past fifteen years I have had on my desk a favorite three-paragraph brevity bearing the above title and using the quote from Psalms. My apologies to the author, the name forgotten. His, however, is a wisdom worthy of sharing and commenting upon. The paragraphs:

The world is not going to the dogs. The human race is not doomed. Civilization is not going to crash. The captain is on the bridge. Humanity is going through a difficult time, but humanity has gone through difficulties many times before in its history, and has always come through, strengthened and purified.

Do not worry yourself about the universe collapsing. It is not going to collapse, and anyway that question is none of your business. The captain is on the bridge. If the survival of humanity depended upon you or me, it would be a poor lookout for the Great Enterprise, would it not?

The captain is on the bridge. God [Infinite Consciousness] is still in business. All that you have to do is to realize the Presence of God where trouble seems to be, to do your nearest duty to the very best of your ability; and to keep an even mind until the storm is over.

As to the verse from Psalms, The New English Bible clarifies the meaning for us: "Peace is the reward of those who love thy law; no pitfalls beset their path." Were people in this and other countries to "love Thy Law"—Truth and Righteousness—there would be peace on earth and good will toward men. To the extent this is achieved, the fewer will be the pitfalls that beset our paths. The author of Thy Law as here dramatized? The Captain on the bridge!

A few individuals—yours truly included—profoundly believe that the world is not going to the dogs, but ever so many are certain that civilization is doomed, that there is no hope. They throw in the sponge, give up the ghost, become drop outs—fold up their tents, as the saying goes.

This unfortunate defeatism is partly spawned by countless fortune tellers: "persons who profess to *foretell* events. . . ." Many of these prognosticators call themselves economists. A few claim to "love Thy Law," but they have lost sight of the Captain on the bridge. Theirs is nothing less than crystal gazing: "the practice of gazing into a crystal ball and *pretending* to see certain images, especially of future events." The truth? They have no crystal ball and couldn't read it if they had one!

No living person has the slightest idea of what is going to happen in the next minute let alone in future decades. The only forecasting that has any validity is of the "iffy" kind. Example: *If* the money supply in the U.S.A. continues to escalate at the same rate as it has from 1935 to 1978, by the year 2000 it will be $1,500,000,000 and the dollar won't be worth a plugged nickel.

The only value of the if-variety of forecasting is alerting citizens to the dangers of over-extended government. Thus alert, they will see to it that government is restored to its proper role of keeping the peace and invoking a common justice. How near or far off is this hoped-for turnabout? I do not know nor does anyone else. But it's the only way to align self with the Captain on the bridge!

True, we are now going through a critical period, but crises are nothing new, as all history attests. However, the instances in which humanity has been "strengthened and purified" are numerous. Reflect on major turnabouts: the Sumerians of 5,000 years ago; Venice during Marco Polo's time; England following the works of Adam Smith, Richard Cobden, John Bright and Frederic Bastiat. The greatest of all followed the brilliant works of our Founding Fathers.[1]

What about right now? Much is going on in the hearts and souls and minds of men—an improved and encouraging awareness—that is invisible to those who only casually glance at surface events. For one of several current examples, have a look at Argentina.[2] The Captain is, indeed, on the bridge!

Why worry about the universe collapsing? As our friend writes—"that question is none of your business." Or mine!

---

[1] See "Eruptions of Truth," in my *Awake for Freedom's Sake,* p. 22.
[2] See my chapter, "Lessons from Afar" in *Vision*, pp. 7-13.

Nor is it necessary to go into outer space to make this point; the earth will suffice. Untold millions in today's world are making it their business to keep civilizations from going to the dogs. By self-improvement? Precisely the opposite: by coercively imposing their plans on Americans, Russians, Chinese and other populations!

To grasp the absurdity of these misguided efforts, imagine that these little dictocrats, rather than the Captain, had been in charge of the evolutionary process since the dawn of earthly life. To aid the imagination, reduce the life scene on planet earth to a single year:

January through August—Traces of worms.
November—Reptiles, dinosaurs, crocodiles, first mammals.
December to 7:00 P.M. on the 31st—First snakes, elephants, deer.
Beginning at 7:00 P.M. of December 31st—First man.
11:50 P.M.—Cro-Magnon man.
11:58:30—*First civilization* (Sumer).
11:59:24—Christ is born.

During the last *three and two-thirds seconds* humanity witnessed the Declaration of Independence, the Constitution and the Bill of Rights. Briefly, freedom in its glory, the furthest advance in the whole life scene! Indeed, it is so new that most people haven't developed the eyes to see this remarkable achievement.

The point is that there would have been no insects or deer had our present-day dictocrats been in charge—not even a worm! Nor would there be any such word as evolution. Yet, human beings in today's world have evolved far above

Cro-Magnon man. Why? Because each human being is free to emerge and grow. Not any one of us, but the Captain, is in charge!

The Great Enterprise is evolution which would be at an end were it dependent upon you or me or any other mortal being. Wrote W. H. Carruth:

> A fire-mist and a planet,
>> A crystal and a cell,
> A jellyfish and a saurian,
>> And caves where the cavemen dwell;
> Then a sense of law and beauty,
>> And a face turned from the clod—
> Some call it Evolution,
>> And others call it God.

It matters not what name we give to Infinite Consciousness—Creation—for we know not what it is, only *that it is!* Let us, then, "realize the Presence of God" and strive as best we can to grow, emerge, *evolve* in the direction of God's Truth and Righteousness!

Let us displace the do-as-I-say way of life with hard work at self-improvement if we would know and enjoy the blessings of freedom.

Thank God, for the Captain on the bridge!

12

TO TOLERATE OR NOT?

There are those who believe something, and therefore will tolerate nothing; and on the other hand, those who tolerate everything because they believe nothing. **—ROBERT BROWNING**

Nearly everyone feels strongly about something. Reflect on the millions who believe in socialism—something—and have no tolerance whatsoever for freedom. And there are those who believe in freedom—an opposite something—who are intolerant of any individual who does not agree with them.

On the other hand, there are numerous wishy-washy types who are barren of any ideological ideas, who will tolerate this or that something, be it socialism or freedom. Thus, we have examples of both intolerance and tolerance—and both wrong! This matter deserves some homework if we freedom devotees are to discover what we should and should not tolerate.

Here is an insight and a foresight recorded by a Danish physician—A. Bartholini (1597-1643)—which offers a bit of enlightenment on the proper and improper uses of tolerance:

> . . . the test of a free society is its tolerance of what is deplored or despised by a majority of its members . . . *free societies are better fitted to survive than closed societies.*

I characterize the above as foresight because Bartholini grasped the truth that a few of us have barely learned from historical examples. This Dane, writing 3½ centuries ago, had never heard of the Sumerian civilization. That first freedom-oriented society—5,000 years ago—wasn't recognized from its dim and buried past until a century ago. Nor did he know about the Venice of Marco Polo's time. He hadn't heard of the Physiocrats, or of the turnabout in England following the work of Adam Smith, Cobden and Bright. He was unaware of the revolutionary concept that the Creator, not government, is the endower of men's rights to life and liberty—the genesis of the American miracle.

Having lectured in Copenhagen and having numerous friends in that country, I learned that Denmark, in spite of many wars and monarchical governments, was in many respects freedom oriented. There was considerable competition and free exchange for several centuries. This explains why Bartholini was aware of the distinction between "free societies" and "closed societies"—between monarchical rule and some freedom being practiced at the same time.

Admittedly, our problem is difficult. Today, in all countries, the vast majority of citizens deplore and despise the private ownership, free market, limited government way of life. To these millions, the free society is abominable, the

closed society admirable. This dislike is common to all
occupational categories. It finds expression from
classrooms—including "economists"—pulpits, business
and labor "leaders" and so on. Cause, indeed, to explore!

That free societies are better fitted to survive than closed
societies is obvious. However, we must distinguish between
what does and does not survive. Is it societies—the
people—or governments of the dictatorial brand?

The historical record gives the unhappy answer loud and
clear: all-out governments! Despotism is the rule—pun
intended! Under dictatorship, how do the people fare? The
answer is—poorly. They starve by the millions as in India
and other countries. In other nations they are slaughtered or
sent to Siberia, or undergo similar calamities. Life span?
Short! Adam Smith reported that in the Highlands of
Scotland, only 200 years ago, it was not uncommon that a
mother had to give birth to twenty children to assure two
reaching adulthood. Such was the poverty and infant mortal-
ity rate!

Now reflect on the few instances where a people's
government has been limited to invoking a common justice
and keeping the peace. These free societies have survived
for relatively short periods. But what about the people in
these rare circumstances? Limited governments leave them
self-responsible and, as a result, they prosper economically,
intellectually, morally, spiritually. Life span? The average
infant in the U.S.A. has a life expectancy of about seventy
years.

According to Bartholini, ". . . the test of a free society is
its tolerance of what is deplored or despised by a majority of
its members. . . ." Why does this present us with a serious

dilemma? A majority of our citizens deplore—even despise—the freedom way of life. These are people who haven't the slightest idea of the miracles that flow from the self-responsibility that limited government assures. Indeed, they are quite content to live off others and barely tolerate the idea that each should attend to his own life and livelihood.

Now reflect on the other side of our ideological coin—on those of us devoted to freedom. Without question, we deplore unlimited government—authoritarianism. But note this: a vast majority on our side of the coin are just as intolerant of those who sponsor the destructive schemes as the opponents of freedom are of us! Intolerance reigns which, if not overcome, makes a free society impossible. How can such a confrontation be resolved?

Obviously, we cannot rid our society of intolerance by setting our opponents straight. The more intolerant we are of them, the more intolerant they will be of us. Who then should we set straight? Ourselves, of course! And what a task this is—ridding the self of traits that are more or less instinctive or inborn. Only reason can come to the rescue.

Phillips Brooks brilliantly stated what your and my ambition should be:

> We anticipate a time when the love of truth shall have come up to our love of liberty, and men shall be *cordially tolerant* and earnest believers both at once.

To love truth, to love liberty, and to be cordially tolerant: these are inseparable parts of a glorious intellectual triumvirate. Reason suggests that not one of these can be omitted without a collapse of the whole. No argument about the love of truth and the love of liberty; being *cordially tolerant* is the debatable issue and the one we should examine.

Samuel Taylor Coleridge, the English poet and critic, writing in 1809, gives us wise counsel: "The only true spirit of tolerance consists in our *conscientious* toleration of each other's intolerance." This is to say that tolerance is never a slipshod or bungling achievement. It has to be conscientious, that is, based on reason of the highest order.

If we wish others to be tolerant, neither you nor I can do much about it except to set a right example. As Burke wrote, "Example is the school of mankind. They will learn at no other."

Assuredly the first step is to realize how far even the best of us is from Infinite Wisdom. Visualize a ladder extending infinitely into space—no ending. If I have advanced, say to the third step, the tendency is to be intolerant of those on the first and second steps—the know-nothings! Were such intolerance warranted, then those on higher steps are equally warranted in being just as intolerant of me; and those on still higher steps intolerant of them. A world full of intolerance and barren of example!

Unless this fault be corrected, beginning with a few examplars, the free society is not possible, for no society can be both free and intolerant. The remedy? An acknowledgment of an incontrovertible fact: Mortal man possesses only infinitesimal grains of wisdom—regardless of how far up the ladder. We humans are mere fledglings!

For anyone to be intolerant of others is to assess himself as the infallible I, *the authority* in rendering final judgments. Such authoritarianism is the very opposite of the freedom one avowedly stands for.

Here are four suggested behavioral attitudes:

- No name calling of opponents or of their doctrines—none whatsoever!
- If a nonbeliever in freedom can't be tolerated, don't drink tea with him, as the saying goes. Confine your association to those who can enlighten you.
- Let those of us who deplore socialism strive for an improved understanding and exposition of freedom. A preoccupation with what's wrong is a waste of the time needed for discovering what's right.
- No individual originates truth. Each is, at best, a receiver of Infinite Wisdom. Thus, life's ambition should be to tune in to as much wisdom as possible. Intolerance tends to turn off one's tuner.

Finally, do not be unhappy or intolerant. Remember, we are ordained to live in the world as it is. Have fun by taking a step or two up that ladder of enlightenment. And as we gain tolerance for our differences, the greater is the chance that freedom may grace our mortal lives!

13

THE CONSERVATION
OF ENERGY

Philosophy should be an energy;
it should find its aim and its ef-
fect in the amelioration [improve-
ment] of mankind.

—VICTOR HUGO

As ever so many are aware, the U.S.A. is experiencing an energy crisis. The reason? Our more or less well-known sources—coal, oil, gas, nuclear—are being energetically controlled by political ordainers—those who order our lives. They know no more about energy than I do! And they are tampering with life's sustenance.

Every form of life manifests energy. No life, be it a blade of grass or a human being, would ever have existed had it not been for this or that variety of energy. This sustainer of life ranges all the way from atomic to solar energy, from waterfalls, to coal, gas and, for all we know, to radiations from outer space. In the absence of energy there would be no life of any kind. Thus, it is supremely important that we learn not only the means by which energy can be conserved, but how to increase it.

Herbert Spencer suggested that the answer must begin with the individual:

It is for *each* to utter that which he sincerely believes to be true; and, adding his unit of influence to all other units, leave the results to work themselves out.

By unit, Spencer refers to such infinitesimal bits of truth as each individual may perceive. No two persons experience identical glimpses of truths. Indeed, no individual's perceptions are precisely the same today as they were yesterday. These tiny bits we experience are in constant flux day in and day out.

When your and my units are added to all the other units, we "leave the results to work themselves out." Of course, they will best work themselves out to the extent that individuals are free from the dictates of those who are unaware of how little they know.

If individuals and their ideas are free of such inhibitions, how will the results work themselves out? Trillions times trillions of tiny bits of expertise *will merge into a truth that is trillions of times greater than that held by any single person.* Trillions of tiny sparks combine into a great and glorious light. This is the most difficult point in politico-economic theory, but once this point is grasped the free and unfettered market comes to light.

Should the free market be permitted to prevail, we would have no more problem with energy than with its sources. The results would be as magic as the causes. Thus, what a wonderful opportunity is opened to the very few who have an awareness of this magic!

The question is, how are the few to cash in on this opportunity? What are the right methods? For, if the tactics be wrong, they will only add to the disaster so heartily deplored.

Victor Hugo passes on to us what amounts to a secret guideline. Solve the energy problem, as other problems, by bringing another form of energy to the rescue: *philosophy!* The following is my way of aiming at the improvement of mankind by calling attention to the wrong ways that the right ways may come to light.

• Forget the "selling freedom" notion! Right method calls for concentration on the improvement of the most approachable person on earth—one's self. This is practical because accomplishment is possible. This tactic disposes of the numbers problem—the impossible, selling the masses.

• Do not seek followers! It is an inordinate waste of time to seek followers. What seek ye then? The achievement of understanding and clarity of explanation, that is, qualities *worth* seeking so that those who wish to learn may come upon enlightenment. If you are successful, those with inquiring minds will find you out. All such achievement is a response to the law of attraction.

• Avoid popular jargon! The language in everyday use is wholly inadequate—more confusing than enlightening— when trying to explain how creativity at the human level works its wonders. Finding words for common sense is an endless chore but it is the task for achievers.

• Avoid anger! Anger has a *dis*tractive rather than an *at*tractive influence. All that one can learn from angry actions is never to use that approach. What then? Have fun! Working for freedom is joyous.

• Be not downcast! As Goethe wrote: "Miracle is the darling child of faith." Pessimists, those who insist that a return to the freedom way of life is hopeless, reduce rather than increase the chances. Success is spawned by the few who sincerely believe that the right will some day prevail. History bears witness to this fact.

• Never resort to name calling! Calling ideological adversaries "fools" or to even think of them as such is to assign that derogatory status to self. True, they do not know very much, nor do the name callers. By calling you a fool, I label myself one. Let criticism be directed at fallacious notions, never at persons!

• Beware of short-run gains! Short-run gains, if not consistent with the long-run objective, take one down the wrong path. A tricky phrase may cause another to say, "I agree." That's a house built on sand; it will quickly fall. Freedom of one and all to work creatively as they please is an eternal verity and should be so understood and explained. Let the long run—eternity—be the guide to human action.

• Do no wrong to anyone! As Confucius declared about 2,400 years ago, "Do not unto others that which you would not have them do unto you." If you are opposed to being plundered and having others dictate how you should live your life, then plunder no one and never attempt to rule over others. This is the oldest and wisest of all maxims—the Golden Rule. When observed, each individual is free to act creatively as he or she pleases—no man-concocted restraints against personal emergence. For freedom's sake, let each of us be an exemplar of the Golden Rule!

- Admittedly, the above suggestions run counter to the views of many freedom devotees. The reason? They observe the advance of socialism through the use of coercive measures. But what they fail to see is that the tactics for destroying a free society are the very opposite of those required to create a free society. Never employ a destructive method to achieve a creative objective!

Finally, our gratitude to Victor Hugo who in his great novel, *Les Misérables* (1862), gave us an invaluable truth: philosophy should be an energy which finds its aim and effect in the improvement of mankind. Here we have an intellectual energy that assures, not only the conservation of those energy forms by which we live and prosper, but their increase. Summarized, this is the freedom way of life!

14

VIOLENCE: THE STRIKER'S TOOL

Where there is no violence, that is, no coercion or intimidation— actual or potential—not a single strike is possible.
—GORDON CONKLIN

A striker is usually depicted as a labor union member willing and able to resort to violence to gain his ends. However, violence as a means of achieving ends is a common occurrence. Strikes are resorted to, more or less, in all walks of life: education, business, even religion—the Crusades, for instance. Persons who try to achieve their objectives by the use of violence or the threat thereof—strikes—are quite illogical in criticizing those who strike back at them. This would be comparable to Hitler's opposing Mussolini on grounds that the latter was a dictator.

Violence is defined as an "unjust use of force of power, as in the deprivation of rights." Violence is an abuse of human rights. In no instance does it properly manifest enlightened self-interest.

Why begin by reflecting on labor union strikes? Because

everyone—those who do and do not participate—are inti-
mately familiar with their use of coercion and/or intimidation. If one can grasp how union violence—an unjust use of
force—is a deprivation of human rights, he will understand
how violence wreaks its damage when employed by politicians or businessmen or whoever.

A labor strike is a refusal to work unless certain conditions of employment are met; but this is by no means the
same thing as quitting a job. The right to quit this or that
employment is one of man's most precious rights. During
the past 70 years—ever since boyhood—I have had not less
than three dozen employments ranging from door-to-door
selling of milk at 3¢ a pint to my present position at FEE.
Two of the jobs turned out to be disagreeable—not liked at
all! Thank heaven I could quit—and did!

Suppose there were no right to quit, stuck for life to a job
assigned by a dictocrat as in Russia—sweeping streets, for
instance. This is to reduce a man to the level of a robot!
What an abuse of human rights!

Nor should we ever question the moral right of workers to
quit in unison, unless this violates a contract. Let all
workers of any employer express their disagreements or
dissatisfactions by simultaneously quitting. Such freedom of
choice should be upheld. Mass quitting does not qualify as a
strike.

What, then, is a strike? It's when violence is brought into
action; *it's when coercion is used to keep others from taking
the jobs that have been vacated!* Here we have freedom of
choice denied to three sets of people: (a) the workers who
would like to stay on the job; (b) the employers who would
like for them to do so; and (c) those consumers who are

deprived of a vital service and denied access to alternative sources of supply. Where there is no violence or intimidation—threats—there is nothing that fits the definition or conditions of a strike.

However, every year there are thousands of strikes not only by workers against business firms but by teachers, engineers, airline captains, stewardesses, longshoremen, on and on. Why this organized depravity? Who knows all the reasons for such ignorance? An inability rationally to interpret self-interest is assuredly one explanation. And doubtless these people are the victims of fashion—strikes being fashionable in our time. As Charles Mackay wrote: "Men, it has been well said, think in herds; it will be seen that they go mad in herds, while they only recover their senses slowly, and one by one."

One of these—a labor union member, for instance—might be able to recover his senses by reflecting on the following example of a strike. Let him go to an M.D. with an ailment. After the examination, the Doctor advises, "You will need to see me for 30 minutes each week over a period of six months." Wondering if he could afford it, the patient asks, "How much?" The Doctor replies, "$10 per visit!" Our worker finds himself in a novel situation: *As a patient he is now the employer; the Doctor an employee.*

On a visit some weeks later, the Doctor announces, "From now on my fee will be $100 per visit. Agree to my demands or I will no longer administer my treatments. Further, our medical union will not permit any other doctor to do so." In other words, no one will be allowed to take the job this doctor has vacated.

The above situation is accurately analogous to the strikes

that daily bedevil our society. Yet, it would be difficult to find a single labor union member who would agree to having done to him that which he advocates and does to others. What an affront to the Golden Rule!

As Emerson wrote, "The end pre-exists in the means." Violence is the means of conducting a strike—an evil means. Equally evil are the results of violence. Furthermore, evil begets evil far more than is commonly realized. Strikes cause others by the countless thousands to strike back; those who are harmed resort to violence as a thoughtless and unjust means of rectifying the damage done to them.

A single example may suffice to illustrate the point. Strikes against a business, whether of short or long duration, cause stoppages in production. The result? No profits for a spell, perhaps even bankruptcy! How do some businessmen redress such a calamity? They solicit government to thwart competition, domestic and/or foreign, by tariffs or embargoes—barriers to free exchange. How enforced? By the governmental police power's use of the same kind of violence exercised by labor unions. The point is that those who strike back in this fashion are in no position to criticize labor union tactics!

What, then, is the appropriate strategy against violence? Condemning the wrongdoers does little good. Instead, explain the folly of violence—regardless of who the practitioners are. That's the first step. The next step is far more important: be a rightdoer one's self. How? Practice and learn to demonstrate with an ever-improving clarity the freedom way of life—the Golden Rule in the politico-economic realm!

To say that one has the right to strike or to strike back is comparable to saying that one endorses monopoly power to exclude competition; it is saying, in effect, that government-like control is preferable to voluntary exchange between buyers and sellers, each of whom is free to accept or reject the other's best offer. In other words, to sanction a right to strike or strike back is to declare that *might makes right*— which is to reject the only foundation upon which civilization can stand.

Lying deep at the root of the strike syndrome is the notion that an employee has a permanent property right in any given job, once he has begun working at it. The notion is readily exposed as false when examined in the above patient-physician relationship. A job is a voluntary exchange of labor for wages, under contract, at terms mutually agreeable to employer and employee. Either party may quit or terminate the job if mutually agreeable terms cease to prevail; but there is no further right to a job that has been vacated.

Those of us inconvenienced and endangered by strikes and counterstrikes are ill-advised to vent our wrath on the participating warriors. Rather, our censure should be directed at the false idea that there is a moral right to strike or to meet violence with violence.

To repeat, violence or the threat thereof is contrary to the enlightened self-interest of everyone and is an abuse of human rights. Instead of organizing strikes and counterstrikes, in an exchange of evil for evil, let us dwell on the virtues of freedom and its unlimited opportunities for one and all!

15

SOCIALISM: LEGALIZED EVIL

The only thing necessary for the triumph of evil is for good men to do nothing.
—EDMUND BURKE

Numerous persons—from Confucius to Henry Hazlitt—have insisted that the only way to capture an idea is to write it out at once; otherwise, like a dream, it is gone forever. I try to follow this counsel, and so I have kept a daily journal for years. Last evening I came across this recording of some 17 years ago, "Socialism is legalized evil," a truth I had forgotten. It was revealed to me by the late Bradford Smith, a brilliant economist and one of the greats among freedom devotees. I am in his debt.

I am also in debt to Edmund Burke for his wisdom. Why is it that millions of *good* men do nothing about the triumph of this particular evil—socialism? In the first place, they do not know what socialism is and, secondly, even if they did know, they would not regard it as evil, so highly is socialism praised in our day and age. They are good men in the limited realm of what they know to be good. All of us have our limited realm.

Good men, in order to do *something* rather than nothing, must know what socialism is. Here is its double barreled definition:

Government ownership and control of the *means* of production: THE PLANNED ECONOMY. Government ownership and control of the *results* of production: THE WELFARE STATE.

Were the title, "Communism: Legalized Evil," many of the good men would readily agree. But they fail to realize that communism and socialism are basically one and the same! The Russians concede this by calling their nation the USSR—Union of Soviet *Socialist* Republics. Furthermore, the term Nazi was a derisive abbreviation of National Socialism. Communism, Nazism, Fascism, the planned economy and the welfare state are modern forms of authoritarianism, differing only in inconsequential details. Socialism is an apt designation for the whole kit and caboodle!

With the above definition in mind, there is no need to question the legality of socialism. Socialism is legal because everything that government does is legal, that is, authorized by law. But not everything government does is right! One definition of "govern" is "to restrain; hold in check." When government is limited to restricting the destructive actions of men—fraud, violence, misrepresentation and the like—and invokes a common justice, it is good rather than evil. The U.S.A. once stood as history's best example of limited government—the model.

Another definition of "govern" is "to exercise authority over; direct; control; rule; manage." This is precisely the kind of governing exercised by socialism. It is nothing more than a modern adaptation of primitive "thinking." And it is as evil as can be!

Good men, when they understand the nature of the Planned Economy and the Welfare State, will see that socialism is evil. And by evil I mean "morally bad or wrong; injurious; bringing misfortune; anything that causes disaster," as my dictionary puts it.

The *means* of production in any economy are creative human energies—such as discoveries, inventions, insights, intuitive flashes, capital formation in the form of savings, physical as well as mental exertions. Is it not true that all creativities have their origin in the individual—no exception? And is it not self-evident, also, that no two individuals are remotely alike in creative abilities? *Each human being is unique!* Because each of us is unique, it is morally wrong to treat people as replaceable parts in the social machinery, mere means for achieving some national plan or other.

The Planned Economy is morally wrong in conception, and it breeds additional wrongs. To illustrate: Some years ago, I described the private ownership, free market, limited government way of life to a candidate for Congress. His rejoinder: "I completely agree with your philosophy but I shall not take that position in my campaign. Were I to do so, I would not be elected." This man chose to bear false witness as do millions of politicians and bureaucrats. Bearing false witness is immoral!

Next, why is the Planned Economy disastrous? Instead of individuals seeking their own creative ventures—each task unique—substitutes take over. Who are they? With some notable exceptions, they are, as mentioned above, the millions of politicians and bureaucrats who choose to bear false witness—immoral "planners" of our lives.

Reduce this political plague to understandable dimensions—you and your son. Now assume that you are as brilliant as any one of the U.S.A.'s top officeholders. How competent would you be to plan your son's way of life, what his creative talents shall be, what he shall invent or discover, the Divine Wisdom he shall intercept? Is it not obvious that you cannot plan even your own future in these respects, let alone your son's? You haven't any more idea of what new thought will grace your soul tomorrow than I have. All of us are faced with the unknown, now and forever.

Reflect on the parents of Confucius or Socrates or Leonardo da Vinci or Mozart or Thomas Edison. These parents knew absolutely nothing of their offspring's oncoming genius. Indeed, these geniuses-to-be did not know what was in store for them!

The Planned Economy is featured by power mongers—bearers of false witness—who haven't the slightest idea of how little they know. They do not even know of your and my existence! Yet, they never question their ability to govern all of us in that primitive, barbaric sense: "to exercise authority over; direct; control; rule; manage." They substitute their know-nothing-ness for the miraculous wisdom of the free and unfettered market—each free to act creatively as he pleases. Limited government? That idea never would occur to one who presumes to know everything, and for precisely the same reason: blindness!

In today's U.S.A. no one can count the ways these dictocrats rule our lives. Their controls range from the shape of toilet seats, to where we shall work and for how much, to what and with whom we may exchange, to what part of our own income we can retain, to countless other utter absurdities.

Any coercive control that squelches anyone's creativity is disastrous. The Planned Economy takes first place and, thus, *it is evil!* Unfortunately, it is also legal.

The second type of socialism is the Welfare State: government ownership and control of the *results* of production. Is this evil? Yes, for it is wrong in conception and it breeds additional wrongs.

All good men will concede that blackmail—"to coerce (into doing something) as by threats"—is evil. Is not the oft parroted Marxist line, "from each according to his ability, to each according to his need" precisely the same evil, that is, when coercively implemented? It is a sin—the breaking of moral law. One of the wisest observations relating to this thesis was written in antiquity—no one knows precisely when. It is from that sacred Hindu text, *The Bhagavad-Gita:*

> Sin is not the violation of a law or convention . . . but ignorance . . . which seeks its own private gain at the expense of others.

It is not only thieves who seek their private gain at the expense of others; millions of good men do likewise—and quite innocently. Reflect on the vast number of people the government pays for not working, or not farming; think of the countless thousands of other private gains at the expense of producers. Even producers fall into this trap, baited with subsidies, restrictions of competition, and so on. Uncomprehending naivete—but evil, nonetheless!

Government produces nothing on its own. If it is to own and control the *results* of production, it must either seize such goods and services from producers or raise the funds with which to purchase them. If direct taxation does not yield sufficient funds, then government will tax indirectly by diluting the medium of exchange—*Inflation!* Additional inflation—legal monetizing of debt—has occurred every year for the past several decades.

All subsidies or giveaways depend upon prior production. If there were no production, there could be no giveaways. That government should have become the instrument of such coercive redistribution is a far cry from the limited role it once served in the U.S.A.

Why do so few good men give so little heed to the present slump into socialism? Because they are enjoying the prosperity that still exists! What they fail to grasp is that our well-being rests solely on the individual creativity that socialism has not yet destroyed!

Assuming that this analysis is reasonably correct, should we be discouraged? Of course not! As Rudolph Steiner counseled, "Try to find the good in the bad. It is always there." For a sample of my findings, see "Out of Evil: Good!"[1] One will then see why I applaud this mess as a necessary steppingstone to the turnabout now in the offing! Confront the true character of socialism squarely and its evil nature is starkly revealed. And then we pray: *DELIVER US FROM THIS EVIL!*

---

[1]See Chapter 24 in my book, *Vision,* pp. 132-138.

16

WHO SHALL RULE
THE RULERS?

*Men are marked out from the
moment of birth to rule or be
ruled.* —**ARISTOTLE**

This remarkable thinker, a pupil of Plato, made the above
observation about 23 centuries ago. While it does not make
much sense to Americans of our time, it was a candid
observation of life in his time. Why? The Greeks of Aristotle's day were born into a rigid caste system from which
there was little escape. To be born a slave committed a
person to that low grade for life. On the other hand, to be
born the son of a ruler made a Greek eligible for rulership.
Politico-economic darkness!

The very opposite of that low grade way of life had its
inception in 1776 with the Declaration of Independence and
the supplementary documents—the Constitution and the
Bill of Rights. Government was limited more than ever
before in history, having nothing on hand to dispense nor
the power to take from some and give to others.

Slavery? Except for that one horrible error imposed on Negroes for a time, it made not one whit of difference as to one's station—rich or poor. A memorable example is a lad born (1809) in abject poverty. "Of formal schooling he had almost none; the scattered weeks of school attendance in Kentucky and Indiana amounted in all to less than a year. *Yet so avid was he for learning that he schooled himself.*"[1] This lad, Abraham Lincoln, became the 16th President of the U.S.A.!

America—the land of the free—with opportunities unlimited! From the time of Lincoln's birth to the present day untold millions have realized their life's ambitions contributing, often unknowingly, to our country's wondrous ascendancy. And a large percentage of these individuals were born in poverty. During my many years of exploring the miracles of freedom, I have been acquainted with ever so many who rose from poverty to become top-ranking leaders in their chosen fields. Whence these unprecedented blessings? Freedom of choice for everyone regardless of birth!

Regrettably, for the past several decades, we Americans have been slumping—sinking into the identical politico-economic bog from which our forebears escaped. From enlightenment to darkness! From a government of strictly limited power to a condition of rulers unlimited. If we are to again get on the right track, we shall have to find the correct answer to *who shall rule the rulers!* More precisely, how shall we curb this ruling passion?

The root of the problem was seen by Tacitus, a Roman historian of about 19 centuries ago: "The desire to rule is

---

[1]See the *Columbia Encyclopedia*, p. 1187.

more vehement than all the passions." The passion for personal riches or fame or notoriety is rarely as vehement as the passion for power to run the lives of others—to rule.

As Burke wrote, "Power gradually extirpates from the mind every humane and gentle virtue." Briefly, the lust for such power stems not from the strength but a weakness of character. Thus the millions of power mongers: weaklings who know not how to run their own lives, although they "know" how to run yours and mine!

Now to our role—what can we do to replace the oncoming darkness with the light of freedom? The answer is as simple to state as it is difficult to achieve: promote an understanding and practice among more and more Americans of an all-too-rare wisdom.

The rare wisdom in question was pronounced by Herodotus, another Greek living two centuries before Aristotle and known as "the father of history." Here it is: *"I desire neither to rule or be ruled."* And these are not twin desires, but one. For every would-be ruler is hopelessly ruled by his desire to rule. To be free, he must free himself of any such desire.

Conceded, the millions incapable of overcoming their passions to rule—dictate how our lives should be lived—are hopelessly lost to our cause. And the same may be said of the millions who prefer a robot status to individuality— being one's own man! On the basis of numbers, the score is at least 100 to 1 on the power monger side. Discouraging? Of course not! Every good movement in the world's history has been led by an infinitesimal minority. May you and I aspire to be among these few!

The Greeks of antiquity continue to enlighten us, not only

by posing social problems but also in making excellent suggestions for their solution. Wrote Epicurus about 22 centuries ago:

The greater the difficulty, the more glory in surmounting it. Skillful pilots gain their reputation from storms and tempests.

This wise man's philosophy prescribed a life of pleasure "regulated by morality, temperance, serenity, and cultural development." What could be a greater pleasure than living in strict accord with this moral premise!

That the power mongers are analogous to storms and tempests is self-evident. Surmounting them is, indeed, difficult. But what greater glory could we experience than getting a few others to share with us the wisdom of wishing neither to rule or be ruled!

Finally, those of us who aspire to the free society can realize our goal only as we (1) understand and obey the basic principles—rules—of morality and ethics, and (2) succeed in limiting civil law to assuring liberty and justice for one and all alike. This is the formula for ruling the rulers out of existence!

17

THE DANGER OF SUCCESS

Success is full of promise till men
get it, and then it is as a last year's
nest from which the bird has
flown. —HENRY WARD BEECHER

Just as I was preparing as moderator to adjourn a weekend
seminar in Wisconsin, a college president interrupted. He
asked, "Isn't it true that the more complex the society, the
more government control we need?" Here is the ensuing
dialogue:

"Joe, let's assume that I am as brilliant as the President of
the U.S.A. How competent would I be to run your life, to
dictate what you should learn, what goods or services you
should produce, how many hours you should work, what
and with whom you should exchange?"

"You would not be competent to do that."

"That is the correct answer. Now, let's assume that I am
to run the lives of the 80 participants at this seminar. What
do you think of that?"

"Utterly absurd!"

"Again a correct answer. Lastly, let's assume that I

80

propose to run the lives of the 200 million citizens of our nation. What's your answer to that?''

''Let's adjourn the meeting.''

''Meeting adjourned.''

This President, a leading ''educator,'' was afflicted with a fallacy typical of the fuzzy notions that afflict a people once successes have come too easily and, thus, are not understood. Would that all such fallacies were as easily disposed of as his! But they are not! Once success is achieved without the reasons being grasped, it is, indeed, like last year's nest from which the bird [understanding] has flown!

Success is not dangerous when we grasp the causes; it is loaded with danger when we are blind to them. Our early ancestors, by and large, knew the causes of success. It was hard work from morning till night—everything from sawing wood to growing and harvesting corn to making candles. The correlation between productive labor and having the wherewithal needed for survival was simple; reward was clearly proportioned to effort. The bird was in the nest!

The bird is no longer in the nest. Why? The early and clearly recognized correlation between labor and productivity—physical and intellectual—served as a springboard for successes today, and so fantastic, that hardly anyone traces the effect back to causes. Only a handful of people are aware of the dangers of such ignorance.

A good example might begin with an observation by an author unknown to me: ''The known is no longer a problem.'' That is to say, once we know how to harness electricity, for instance, its power is available to serve a variety of purposes. But what about the unknown? Reflect on what has happened in this single field of electricity since the days of Benjamin Franklin: there have been so many discoveries that no human being is aware of more than an infinitesimal fraction of them. Typical, is a new telephone system just installed at FEE. The heart of it is an electronic switching panel having hundreds of thousands of transistorized circuits. How many know the causes of this fantastic wonder? Few indeed.

There are millionaires by the thousands who haven't the slightest idea as to why they are wealthy. Day laborers? I have just read of a beer company where ordinary workers receive salaries of $21,000 annually. What a contrast to a job of mine over 60 years ago! The pay? Five cents an hour! How easy for me to learn the connection between hard work and productivity! The above-mentioned beer workers typify millions of workers in all walks of life who are utterly unaware of this relationship. Confusion reigns! We must know why and the form these dangers take. If this can be done, perhaps the remedy will be clear.

The above must not be taken as approving the labor theory of value—the worst of all fallacies having to do with economic theories. Omitted for brevity's sake are the first causes of economic success: capital formation and free exchange. Generally understood? By about as many as know how to produce Grand Operas! Free exchange is giving ground to forced exchange, and the results are dangerous, indeed! Some reflection on the form these dangers take would seem to be in order.

Here are three observations that should be self-evident:

- We are the most advanced division-of-labor society that has ever existed.

- We are more specialized than any people have ever been.
- Thus, no people have ever been further removed from self-sufficiency than present-day Americans!

For example, I do not know how to raise the many varieties of food I consume, to build the house I live in, to make the clothes I wear or the car I drive, to generate electricity or get gas from Texas used for heating and cooking in New York—on and on!

To confirm this situation, merely imagine how well you would fare were you to live only on that which you now do or even know how to do. You would perish! And so would all Americans!

The absolute impossibility of self-sufficiency—no one can any longer go it alone—sheds light on an incontrovertible fact: We—all of us—are *interdependent!* Individual survival depends upon *the free, uninhibited exchanges of our specializations!* There are several hundred million specializations, for each individual has a bit of unique expertise, and ever so many have two or more specialties.

Another self-evident fact: Primitive barter cannot be relied upon as a means of effecting exchanges in a highly specialized society. Merely reflect on the absurdity of trying to exchange *The Freeman* for a set of golf clubs, or chickens for an airplane seat, or a painting for a gallon of gasoline, or any one of countless specializations for all the other these and thats. Impossible! What then?

Instead of primitive barter, our highly specialized society requires *a medium of exchange:* money. When honest, money works infallibly, no one giving its workability a second thought; productivity increases and exchanges multiply. However, when the causes of our miraculous economic ascendancy are not understood, inflation—a dilution of the medium of exchange—sets in. Printing money is easier than producing goods, and today inflation is on the rampage!

Why this monetary nonsense? Millions of unaware citizens regard the enormous aggregate of marketable goods and services as a huge grab bag to be plundered. How is this plundering "financed"? By the issuance of so-called legal tender, that is, by fiat or irredeemable paper money: inflation.

The millions who coercively take the fruits of your and my labor unto themselves are not only unaware of the causes of economic affluence but they are equally unaware of the sin they commit. Theirs is the sin of ignorance. Can this be enlightened? Finding explanatory words is our problem—words that will "strike home."

In a previous essay I coined the acronym: LOOT—*L*iving *O*ff *O*thers *T*houghtlessly.[1] Who wouldn't shy away from being known as a looter? The few who understand the detail here at issue gave this essay their approval, ordering many copies. The sinners? To my knowledge, no effect!

So let's try *hold ups* as a descriptive term for what's going on. Strikes are not only legal, but they are unbelievably popular. Yet a strike is no less a hold up than the action of a robber with a gun: "Give us higher wages with *your money* or your company is out of business." That dictate, backed by force, is equivalent to the use of a gun. But not many

---

[1] See my book, *Vision*, pp. 14-19.

union members would like to think of themselves as robbers.

Name a field of activity in which hold ups are not a feature. Embargoes or tariffs are no less hold ups than strikes; they are resorts to force as a means of *killing* competition. Rent control, the Gateway Arch and literally thousands of other examples of getting one's way at the expense of others are hold ups.

Perhaps the most striking and incongruous example is to be found among the clergy—individuals who claim the Holy Bible as their guide. Merely reflect on the countless thousands of them who, from their pulpits, advocate all sorts of political interventions—from social security, to public housing, to progressive income tax. Ordained preachers who advocate this and that form of socialism display no understanding of Exodus 20:15, "Thou shalt not steal." *This Commandment undeniably presupposes private ownership.* The idea of stealing that which is *not* owned is absurd; and stealing that which *is* owned is a hold up.

Henry Ward Beecher was certainly right when he observed that success is full of promises—till men get it! And our fantastic successes will continue to be a politico-economic threat unless we succeed in putting the bird back in the nest—that is, regain an understanding of the causes of ownership and free exchange.

Your and my responsibility is to put that bird back in the nest. To the extent that we succeed will our country regain the title: *land of the free* and home of the brave—brave enough to stand for freedom!

18

PROBLEMS MIRACLES POSE

A miracle is a work exceeding the power of any created agent, consequently being an effect of divine omnipotence.

—ROBERT SOUTH

A miracle, according to the dictionary, is "thought to be due to supernatural causes," or, as the English clergyman, South, has it, "divine omnipotence." All miracles do, indeed, exceed the power of any created agent, that is, any man past or present. And unless a divine source or cause of miracles is recognized, the resultant confusion can lead to chaos—a point that requires some explaining!

My son and I were peering out of an airport window at a 747 jet and I wondered aloud what George Washington would have said had he seen this miracle. Responded my son, "I'll never touch another drop!"

The Father of our country never saw an airplane and perhaps never dreamed of one. Yet he, along with a few other patriots, embraced a fundamental and profound truth which they set forth in the Declaration of Independence. I believe this spiritual truth is responsible for the 747 jet and millions of other miracles.

These spiritual and intellectual exemplars did not have material miracles in mind but only moral and ethical principles that would permit Americans to be self-responsible—each his own man! They sought an escape from the kind of authoritarian rule that had, with few exceptions, plagued societies since the dawn of history. The truth they discovered correlates with the supernatural or God or Infinite Consciousness or the Creator—call the Divine Omnipotence what you will. And here it is, *the very essence of Americanism:*

—that all men are . . . endowed by their Creator with certain Unalienable rights, that among these are Life, Liberty and the pursuit of Happiness.

Here we have the greatest wisdom ever written into a political document. It unseated government as the endower of men's rights and placed the Creator there!

It is one thing to write such a revolutionary concept but quite another matter to implement it—put it into practice. There followed a few years later the Constitution and the Bill of Rights. These limited government more severely than ever before in history—hardly any organized force standing against the release of creative human energy.[1] Government was so limited that it had nothing on hand to dispense nor the power to take from some and give to others!

When citizens cannot turn to government for security, welfare or prosperity, to whom or what do they turn? To themselves! Result? Self-reliance and the greatest outburst of creative energy ever known—miracles by the millions. It is important to keep in mind that the genesis of these

---

[1]For an excellent detailing of the "no's" and "not's" see "Constitutional Restraints on Power" by Edmund A. Opitz (*The Freeman,* April, 1978).

miracles was not the deliberate intent to effect a miracle; they were the fruits of a heavenly principle: that man's rights are the endowment not of government but of the Creator—*the exclusive source of all creativity!*

Comments on a single miracle—the airplane—will make my point. George Washington would have stood in awe of the Wright brothers' first plane, which did no more than leave the ground and flutter in the air for a few moments. Move ahead a few generations and imagine his astonishment had he witnessed the fantastic performance of one of the planes I rigged in World War I—the Sopwith Camel.

Suppose he could have foreseen the 747 jet, that miracle with about 5,000,000 parts; and no one knowing how to make a single one of them! Who can imagine his reaction to this glory of the heavens! Transportation at 500-600 miles per hour as compared with his fastest—on horseback. This miracle of ours can fly around the world in about the time it took him to ride from Mount Vernon to Jefferson's home—a mere hundred miles. Interestingly, Washington and his compatriots, *unknowingly,* set the stage for that jet and millions of other miracles!

No one can foresee the blessings that will flow from human actions if the premise be right. Our Founding Fathers received from a heavenly source and bestowed on their countrymen the best politico-economic premise ever written. Assume that we return to an understanding and strict observance of that righteous premise—presently all but forgotten. Should we do so, I can no more imagine the miracles 200 years in the future than Washington could have foreseen the 747 jet. Nor can you or anyone else!

As no one knows how to make a simple pencil or a single

part on an airplane, so no one now knows or ever has known how to write the righteous premise. In either case, it is an interception of what Emerson called "immense intelligence"—Creation. Thus, if intellectual and material progress is to grace us, we must accept and abide by the incontrovertible fact that the source of all benefactions is Divine Omnipotence, not elected and appointed officials—government. Even as brilliant a President as George Washington could no more write and act out an eternal truth than he could make an airplane. Would he agree? Here is his answer: "Let us raise a standard to which the wise and honest can repair. *The event is in the hand of God.*"

Our miracles bump into several obstacles or obstructions—which we must understand and overcome. First and foremost are the false opinions which millions of political dictocrats have of themselves. They see themselves as the very opposite of what they are. These naive and vain persons at all levels of government who are unaware of the moral principles that made America great—the source of all creativity—think of themselves as *the source* of miracles.

Again, let the airplane serve to illustrate their dangerous error. They dictate who can own and operate airlines. No one is free to try; he is only permitted—if the bureaucrats approve. Schedules are coercively determined and so is the question of what airports are open to entry. The same goes for passenger and freight rates. Airports are owned and controlled by governments—on and on.

Regardless of these obstacles, the performance of airlines is miraculous. And the dictocrats in their blindness take the credit! Actually, their intervention and control only limits—forestalls—millions of additional miracles that would otherwise be wrought were the free and unfettered market allowed to function. Unless these regulators are divested of their present power, miracles will, sooner or later, be no more than phenomena of the past!

What of those outside the political hierarchy—those who experience discoveries, inventions, insights, intuitive flashes? Persons so graced are to be found in every walk of life, regardless of occupation, race or nationality.

Most of these individuals interpret their contributions to the miraculous as originating in their own minds, unaware that their insights are but interceptions of Divine Omnipotence. As a consequence, they regard their little think-of-thats as personal property, no less than their homes, autos, pay checks or whatever.

By and large, they defend such error as vigorously as they would defend their home against thieves. The discovery or invention is their property, or so they "think"! The forms of defense are countless. A mere sampling: Businessmen fight for tariffs, embargoes and the like; others seek licenses or patents or copyrights or exclusive franchises or some other form of protectionism!

What kind of thinking can bring about a corrective procedure? It must begin with an acknowledgment that every one of these think-of-thats—no exception—is but an interception of the flow of Infinite Consciousness; therefore, any individual who intercepts this or that is no more than a fortunate intermediary!

Patents, for instance: It is a safe guess that more than 99% of all think-of-thats contributing to the miraculous have not been patented. And copyrights? "All truly wise ideas have been thought already thousands of times." True, we copyright our monthly journal, *The Freeman*. Why? Only to secure a Library of Congress catalogue number. Note, however, that we permit reprints without request. Briefly, knowing that our works are but interceptions, we wish them to freely flow—share and share alike!

Imagine what would happen if each of us were to share the ideas he intercepts, regarding ourselves as transmitters—not possessors—of the heavenly flow. There would be at least two immediate blessings:

- It is an observed fact that the more we share the more and higher grade are the ideas we receive.
- The resulting miracles would be far more numerous than we can imagine. There would be intellectual enrichment and prosperity would grace the citizenry!

Why an intellectual enrichment? When people have no awareness of *The Source,* wealth goes to their heads, makes "softies" of them. They give no thought to the problem wealth presents. Instead of solving this and related problems themselves, they refer them to Washington or to some other political body, unaware that political bodies have no competence in this respect—none whatsoever!

However, when Divine Omnipotence is recognized as the source of miracles, the individual finds his place in the Cosmic Design. He is aware that his role is to solve problems—not transmit them into the political arena. This attunement with Creation is the greatest of all intellectual enrichments!

These intellectually enriched individuals never regard wealth as an end in itself. They see wealth as only a means to freeing oneself from the mundane chores of life so that all his hours and days and years may be devoted to interceptions, perceptions—*Creativity!*

19

HOLLOW OR
HALLOW DAYS?

The holiest of all holidays are those
Kept by ourselves in silence and apart,
The Secret anniversaries of the heart,
When the full river of feeling overflows;—
—LONGFELLOW

It was Friday evening preceding this year's Memorial weekend. To the airline hostess who was writing tickets to Toronto for FEE's seminar team, I remarked, "There should be no *legal* holidays." Her response, "You are grouchy." Doubtless others will think likewise about my criticism of this very old, popular and destructive governmental intervention. The question: Can the case be made that *legal* holidays are no more than hollow days?

The two main themes I intend to stress are:

(1) The declaration of a legal holiday is basically a coercive transfer payment—full pay without work—a tax upon the employer to provide a benefit payment to the

92

employee. It is a cost of hiring labor, a cost of doing business, forcibly imposed by government.

(2) The second theme is more a question: Is a coercively imposed legal holiday the appropriate way to celebrate the great person or great idea or great event that is important to us in this land of the free?

Believing in freedom of choice, I have no quarrel with others taking time off for a day, week, month, year or forever. That's their business and, thus, no concern of mine. But the nigh unanimous approval or *legal* holidays deserves a careful assessment. So let's go around the calendar—January through December.

New Year's Day is a *legal* holiday. This year another long weekend! As with several other holidays, the Federal government, with labor union insistence, dictates long weekends. Why? To shorten the work week! What happens? Millions of people get into their cars and jam the highways, going and coming at the same time. Hundreds are killed! That cuts *their* work week to zero, now and forever. A *legal* New Year's Day is, indeed, a hollow day—destructive and hollow of thought.

The thoughtful person will think of January 1st as any other day and go or come back as one would on the 5th or 10th or whatever. Regard it as no more than the first day of the rest of life, and make it the best of all the days so far lived!

February 12—Lincoln's birthday—is a legal holiday but no stoppage of work on Mondays. The schools do not close and the traffic is normal. This man—one of the greatest—if his thinking be understood aright—would be pleased that his fame has not brought on infamous actions.

George Washington—February 22—has had his birthday legalized at whatever date most nearly approximates a weekend that gives the most time off from work. People are killed by the hundreds every year in his honor!

Next, reflect on how little thought—if any—is given by the holidaying millions to Washington's part in founding the greatest nation in all history. He was as much the founder of freedom way of life as anyone who has lived! Legalizing a holiday to the Statue of Liberty would accomplish as much in intellectual, moral and spiritual advancement—nothing!

Move on to another legal Hollow Day—Memorial Day—originally celebrated in the North on May 30th and in the South on April 26th, May 10th or June 3rd. It was inaugurated in 1868 for the purpose of decorating the graves of Civil War veterans, that war a national disgrace! The loss of lives in 1978 during this prolonged weekend? Five hundred and forty-two fatalities on the highway and one hundred and thirty drownings! What a way to decorate graves!

If we were really interested in doing honor to those who have lost their lives in wars between nations, we should regard every day as a *Hallow* (holy) Day. How? Do all possible to replace bureaucrats in international affairs with free traders, the latter being the only ambassadors of good will and peaceful relationships between nations.[1]

Independence Day—the Fourth of July—is a perfect example of how futile and even harmful is any effort to advance high ideas and ideals by merely legalizing a day.

Why Independence Day in the first place? To celebrate the adoption of the Declaration of Independence, the greatest politico-economic document ever written! The aim was laudable; the method—a legal holiday—is deplorable! High ideals

---

[1]For a commentary on the Civil War and how to strive for peace, see the chapter, "War and Peace" in my book, *Awake for Freedom's Sake.*

are never achieved by statist intervention, a denial of freedom to choose.

The high ideal—the very essence of Americanism:

—that all men are endowed by their Creator with certain unalienable Rights, that among these are Life, Liberty and the pursuit of Happiness.

This year, the Fourth of July is on a Tuesday. Millions of citizens will be on the highways by Friday evening, returning to work Wednesday morning. Why is this "weekend" four hollow days? It is no more than a funfest—vacationing.

True, this may be some people's idea of the pursuit of happiness—no work and all play. However, not one in thousands will give the slightest thought to the significance of accepting the Creator rather than government as the endower of our rights!

A vast majority in today's U.S.A. are unaware of a single line in the Declaration. Were Independence Day not legalized—everyone having freedom of choice—it is a fair guess that many would honor this occasion by either teaching or learning about *the very essence of Americanism—the source of the American miracle!*

Labor Day tops the list of my unfavorite hollow days. Why is it always on Monday? The reason should be clear: fewer hours of labor for some 20 million labor union members—and getting paid for their time off!

John Ruskin passed on to us an enlightened assessment of labor:

It is only by labor that thought can be made healthy, and only by thought that labor can be made happy, and the two cannot be separated with impunity.

But when labor and thought are coercively separated, the price is unbelievably high. Every person who works—whatever the occupation—is a laborer. There are some 70 millions of us who work but are not members of labor unions!

Can we at FEE work on Labor Day? Not as we usually do! The government post office is closed—no mail. Those around the nation we might wish to contact by phone are off for the Labor Day weekend—their offices closed. So far as our labors are concerned, Labor Day is a deadened day!

For me, there is no greater joy in life than my labor. May I and others celebrate the bringing together of labor and thought—day in and day out—as we freely choose!

Thanksgiving Day had its beginning in 1621. Those Pilgrims still alive, following a winter of starvation and privation, gave thanks to the Lord for their blessings.

But as a legal hollow day, Thanksgiving is now featured by feasting and away for a gay old time—Thursday, Friday, Saturday and Sunday. How many in today's America bow their heads in prayer acknowledging blessings the Pilgrims couldn't even imagine? Few, indeed!

The rightful alternative to this legal hollow day? Count one's blessings every day in the year—a daily thanksgiving, each a *hallow* (holy) day!

Finally, what about Christmas, the day we celebrate the birth of our Perfect Exemplar? Legalized, what do we observe? Far more shopping than worship, the stores more crowded than churches, traffic more in evidence than people striving to approximate His Exemplarity!

Being told by those in political office—a good number being atheists—when to strive for religious perfection is more stultifying than encouraging. So why not do away with this intervention and let Christians and those of other religions pay their homage today, tomorrow—ever and ever!

Acknowledged, we should pay our deepest personal respects to the thinking and contributions to our country by the statesmen, Abraham Lincoln and George Washington. Great men! But reflect on other geniuses, for instance, Emerson, Edison and Henry Wadsworth Longfellow.

What would have been Longfellow's reaction had his birthday been made a *legal* holiday? Unorthodox as mine! Life's ascendancy is a private matter—a personal striving for Truth and Righteousness, "the secret anniversaries of the heart."

If we are to restore the freedom way of life to our beloved America, let all individuals be free to make each day a *Hallow*—holy—Day. Such would be "The holiest of all holidays."

20

ELEMENTARY EDUCATION

*Look out for the boy who has to
plunge into work direct from the
common school and who begins
by sweeping out the office. He is
probably the dark horse you had
better watch.*
—ANDREW CARNEGIE

The above observation was made by one of our country's
greatest entrepreneurs. In contrast, here is a decree uttered
by Napoleon, one of the world's noted dictators: "Public
instruction should be the first object of government."
Would I rather be born the poor boy with work as a
necessity or a Napoleon with unlimited power and the
wealth of a nation at my command? A sweeping boy, by far!
And for understandable reasons.

As an introduction to this thesis, let me recall a story told
about Alexander the Great. Leading his armed forces
through the countryside, Alexander was informed by his
aide that the world's greatest philosopher was meditating on
the hillside. Alexander went to the philosopher and began

boasting about how great he was, how powerful, and offered to grant any wish the philosopher might have. After listening to the "great" know-it-all, the philosopher remarked, "Please move aside; *you are standing between me and the Sun!*"

The curt request, "Move aside; you are standing between me and the Sun," might also come appropriately from a child in the first grade. All philosophical achievers have had their beginnings in elementary education of this or that variety. Reflect on the obstructions to human progress—creativity in its countless forms—were education limited to Napoleonic tactics with some know-it-all in the educational driver's seat! There would be no philosophers, no righteousness, no geniuses; only a world populated with programmed robots. Of all the persons never to emulate is the person so naive as to believe we should be like him or her.

All education is, in fact, elementary—assessments to the contrary notwithstanding. Most individuals think of themselves as educated if they have graduated from high school or college. The fact? Even those with honorary degrees or Ph.D.'s are still at the primary level—first graders—as related to the Infinite Unknown.

Look to the Sun—truth and righteousness—not only as a child, but during every moment of earthly existence. Those on the right course will discover and abide by that Socratic wisdom: The more one knows, the more he or she knows there is to know—the more aware that all is elementary!

Public, that is, government education in the U.S.A. may very well have had some of its roots in Napoleon's dictatorial views such as: "Public instruction should be the first object of government." And this:

Napoleon now merged the various institutions of higher learning in a new University of France *under officials nominated and supervised by the executive power. . . ."* "No one," it was decreed, "may open a school or teach *publicly unless he is a member of the imperial university. . . ."*[1]

If that be the root, then this may be the sequence of its transplanting here. Our brilliant Thomas Jefferson invited his close friend, the brilliant Pierre Samuel du Pont de Nemours, to study and recommend an appropriate form of education for the U.S.A. Du Pont wrote a 161-page book,[2] and Jefferson proceeded to implement its conclusions. Public education!

Why du Pont, a physiocrat and at odds with Napoleon on every other matter, should arrive at such a recommendation is difficult to understand, except that he lived a good part of his life in that "educational" atmosphere. Neither Jefferson nor his friend could see the scraggy bush that would grow from these roots.

The scraggy bush did not show up until well into the twentieth century. But now it is growing by leaps and bounds—and so are costs. In a district not far from FEE the taxpayers are forced to pay about $4,000 per student for nine months of "schooling."

This is not to suggest that all teachers in government schools are indoctrinating students with socialistic non-

---

[1] See *History of Western Education* by William Boyd (London: Adam & Charles Black, 1950), p. 360.

[2] *National Education in the United States of America* (Newark, Delaware: University of Delaware Press, 1923).

sense. There are thousands among the millions of teachers who believe in and explain the blessings of freedom. The Dean of one of our country's largest government universities, for example. During his last year, this man taught a class of seniors, all about to become teachers. He purchased 100 volumes of my book, *The Coming Aristocracy,* gave each senior a copy as required reading and asked for a 2-page, typed evaluation within three weeks. After the papers had served his purpose, he let me see them. Several of the papers were well prepared; but I was astounded at the number of budding teachers who couldn't spell words or construct sentences.

I entered the first grade in a small-town *public* school long before the scraggy bushes had grown—1905. Our teacher for the first four grades was Patience McGinn, an appropriate name—rhyming with "begin," my beginning. She was brilliant, even teaching mental arithmetic which, today, most college professors of mathematics rarely try. And I well remember the few other teachers for the next seven years who, without exception, were remarkably capable. The coercive aspects of government education had not yet set in to bedevil public education. In those days it seemed right, not at all at odds with Jefferson's and du Pont's expectations.

There is, however, more to elementary education than going to school. Prior to my father's passing in 1909, I walked about two miles to school, delivering milk to numerous customers on the way. By so doing, I learned the relationship between hard work and a quart of milk. That's one reason why I am grateful for being born a poor lad rather than a Napoleon. Ever so many of us in those days were schooled by the discipline of work, which is so much more advantageous than being born a dictator.

Thank heaven, child labor laws were not enforced in my day. Otherwise, following my father's demise, I would not have been able to work 102 hours a week, doing farm chores, tending the village store, sweeping it every morning and waiting on customers till 9 P.M. Monday through Friday, to midnight on Saturday, and Sunday forenoon.

Another blessing for which I shall be forever grateful: there were no minimum wage laws. One summer I worked 60 hours every week, my pay being $3.00 for all those hours. Today, that's about the minimum wage for one hour's work! Poor lads, back then, loved every minute of such elementary education.

Today, by reason of the scraggy bushes full grown, criticism of "education" in the U.S.A. is rampant, as much by socialists who do not know the causes, as by freedom devotees who do. The socialists are not against government—socialistic—education. It is their ideal and, thus, they concentrate their "thinking" on how to make socialism work. That's akin to seeking the products and services of work without working!

It would be difficult to find any better explanation for the rapid decline into politico-economic socialism than our socialistic "education"—the scraggy bushes full grown. And, perhaps the remedy cannot begin otherwise than by replacing Napoleonic with elementary education. Were Jefferson and du Pont alive today, I believe they would agree.

Your responsibility and mine is of three parts:

To grasp where lies the responsibility for the education of our children.

To see the utter futility of coercion in education such as compulsory attendance, government dictated curricula and the compulsory collection of the wherewithal to pay the school bills.

To understand how the free market works its wonders in education as it does in goods and services. That's where the wisdom is.[3]

It so happens that I agree with Andrew Carnegie: "Look out for the boy [or girl] who has to plunge into work." Each is "the dark horse you had better watch." Blessings on them! They are the root of what's good, a root that will grow not into a scraggy bush but will bloom into a beautiful tree.

---

[3]For my detailed explanation of these three points, see Chapters 15, 16, 17 in *Anything That's Peaceful*.

21

IN SEARCH OF MYSTERIES

The philosopher aspires to explain away all mysteries, dissolve them into light. Mystery, on the other hand, is demanded and pursued by the religious instinct; mystery constitutes the essence of worship.

—HENRY FREDERIC AMIEL

At the outset, an acknowledgment: I am not a philosopher, at least as that remarkable Swiss critic, Amiel, uses the term. I no more aspire to explain away mysteries than to paint a portrait of God or describe what Creation is. What, then, is an appropriate aspiration for personal life? Growth in consciousness—the one reality, the only aspect of man that is immortalized!

What is the clearest signal that the individual is growing in consciousness? Evidence that he or she is standing more and more in awe of everything—when mysteries are on the increase!

Those who demand and pursue mysteries are graced with the religious instinct, as Amiel asserts. These few, quite naturally, are growing in awareness or consciousness; working with that portion of the self which does not perish. They experience eternal life!

Note that in our mortal moments we are *gifted* with obstacles to overcome. Most people think of day-to-day obstacles as nuisances rather than blessings. These difficulties, however, are steppingstones to becoming. Briefly, we live our mortal moments in the obstructed universe; afterward in the Unobstructed Universe.[1] We enter the latter to the level of consciousness we achieve in the former. Jerome Ellison, in his latest book, shares his findings:

> The purpose of the total creation, and of the human life that flourishes within it, is the evolution of consciousness. The whole evolutionary progression, from gas, to stone, to crystal, to one-celled organism, to plant, to animal, to man and beyond, reveals its single-pointed striving toward ever higher, broader, and deeper capacities for being *aware,* that is, for consciousness.
>
> Mankind today has given itself over to crisis-living, making a great to-do in its press and media about this "crisis" or that—the petroleum crisis, the atomic bomb crisis, the population crisis, the food crisis, and so on. Actually, humanity has only one crisis, a crisis of consciousness. To the most highly evolved minds of our species, ready solutions are already known to all the "crises" just named. The only thing that prevents their adoption is the fact that the mass human mind is still operating at too low a level of awareness to accept them.
>
> The human evolutionary thrust, Julian Huxley has re-

---

[1] See *The Unobstructed Universe* by Stewart Edward White (New York: E. P. Dutton & Co., Inc., 1940).

minded us, has long since passed beyond new experiment in bodily form. Physically, we have been about as we are for many millennia, and will probably remain so. The evolutionary spearhead has transferred its thrust to *psychosocial* evolution, the evolution of consciousness. Therefore, if you want to realize the ultimate meaning of your life, awaken your sleeping faculties to a new effort of exploration of new ideas, new thoughts, new dimensions, new possibilities. Expand your consciousness, that is, *evolve.*

As soon as you begin to take even the first few tentative steps in this direction, a new self-confidence flows into your being. Self-confidence is not having everything hunky-dory, or "having it made." It is not an easy chair where you sit or a house you live in. Self-confidence is a road you travel. It is knowing you are on the right track, regardless of what way stations labeled "success" or "failure" you may pass along the way. When you are evolving your consciousness you are in tune with the all encompassing purpose of the cosmos; you are in harmony with the universe. You are on the right track. Knowing this, you live with a new self-confidence, *élan,* and poise.

We have already noted that a clue is something a detective uses to solve a case. But clues need to be followed up or the case remains unsolved. These, then, are the four clues to radiant living:

1. Know Yourself.
2. Be Yourself.
3. Trust the Infinite
4. Evolve.[2]

---

[2]The above five paragraphs are from an enlightening book, *Life's Second Half* by Jerome Ellison (Old Greenwich, Conn., The Devin-Adair Co., 1978), pp. 167-168.

Growth in consciousness can best be described as a growing awareness of mysteries: the more we know the more we know we do not know. Why is it that so few of us are aware of how little we know? Is it not because our awareness is so infinitesimal that we can barely recognize the tiny stage we occupy!

Reflect on the time when our planet was no more than a hot glob of gas. Its origin? No one has the slightest idea—mystery! A one-celled organism is composed of atoms, but what's an atom? Total mystery! A plant? No one even knows why grass is green—mystery! Move up the scale of Life: oysters to chimpanzees to men. The higher is less tied down to its environment, and the more does freedom of choice prevail.

Ortega wrote, "A tiger cannot become untigerish." But humans can become as inhuman as they choose; or, if perceptive enough, can become truly human. If sufficiently advanced in consciousness, humans will concede that everything in the Universe—no exception—is mystery! At this elevated stage, man "is in tune with the all-encompassing purpose of the Cosmos"—harmony!

Does mystery constitute the essence of worship? Yes; striving for and praying for attunement with Creation, grasping the fact that all is mystery, constitutes the very essence of worship. Thanks for that thought, Amiel.

Finally, let us thank Jerome Ellison for his observation: *"To the most highly evolved minds of our species,* ready solutions are already known to all the 'crises' just named" (the petroleum crisis, the atomic bomb crisis, the population crisis, the food crisis, and so on).

What are the "ready solutions" to which he refers? Strict

adherence to the various components of the free and unfettered market:

- Government limited to keeping the peace and invoking a common justice, that is, inhibiting all destructive actions.
- Private rather than government ownership.
- Freedom for all citizens to produce whatever goods and/or services they please and to exchange with whomever they choose.
- No man-concocted restraints against the release of creative human energy in any field, be it the religious, educational, the economic, or whatever.

How many people adhere to, understand and can explain with clarity why freedom performs its miracles? To my knowledge, not one! For instance, it is easily demonstrable that no one knows how to make a simple wooden lead pencil. Why do we have them in abundance? We leave their production to the market where the wisdom is.

We do not know *what* Creation is, only *that* it is. When every person is free to act creatively as he chooses this is creation at the earthly level, and the results are miraculous. Evolved minds recognize that the remarkable manifestations of individual liberty are no less mysterious than Creation itself.

That's why freedom is a mystery!

22

THE PLEASURES OF AGING

While one finds company in him-
self and his pursuits, he cannot
feel old, no matter what his years
may be.
—AMOS BRONSON ALCOTT

Some forty years ago Walter B. Pitkin, Professor of Philosophy, Columbia University, wrote a book, *Life Begins at Forty.* Very impressive!

Ten years ago I reached the traditional three score years and ten. *Science of Mind* magazine published an article of mine, "Life Begins At Seventy." Professor Pitkin's widow read the article and wrote that her husband would have completely agreed.

The copyright date of this, my 24th book, is September 1978, coinciding with my 80th birthday. Why do I pay a personal tribute to this date? It is because each year since 1933—45 years ago—has had a happier beginning than the previous year. I have indeed experienced the pleasures of aging, so why not a few comments on the thought that life begins at 80? If that date be realized, I shall write into my Journal, "How wonderful to be going on 81" and immediately afterward write *80 of my countless blessings*—a procedure I have followed for years.

Before beginning this brevity I did some research as to what wise men over the centuries have had to say about aging. To my surprise, most of them were gloomy, distraught—the prospect of old age deadening! My own view is just the opposite: to be 80 years young is far better than to be 19 years old!

Alcott, quoted above, was an agreeable exception. The older one is, the more joy there is in exploring the not-yet-known. As for me, no pursuit gives greater pleasure than delving ever deeper into the freedom way of life.

As age progresses, hobbies of earlier years—golf, curling and cooking—have become mere pastimes. Trying to understand the economic, intellectual, moral and spiritual underpinnings of human freedom is now the one inspiring ambition. Thus, regardless of years, I do not feel old, for no one is ever too old to be instructed. As Cervantes wrote, "One must live long in order to see much."

Why is this my favorite book? Not because it is any better than previous books, but because it is the latest! Each of these twenty-two chapters has been written as I approach my 80th birthday. My previous book, *Vision,* also was written and published during the past twelve months! Further, no let-up in travel, seminars, and the many chores at FEE. Continued participation in such pleasurable labors frees one from all fret about the discouraging prospects that the senior years have a tendency to impose. Longevity's purpose, if seen aright, is learning, not lengthening. Wrote someone, "One does not *grow* old. One *becomes* old by not growing."

We should not, it seems to me, associate life's beginning with any particular year; life begins at each and every moment when growth in awareness, perception, consciousness is experienced. Assessed in this manner, many lives come to an end in the teens, while others accelerate into the nineties. If eighty seems less likely than forty for a new beginning, the reason is that a tombstone has been erected over the aspiration to grow.

Why do I find so many pleasures in aging? By reason of thoughts originating with me? Indeed, not! From whom? From those I have been fortunate enough to choose as tutors—the thoughts I have gleaned from their books. So let me share some of these thoughts.

The researches of Roger Williams, professor of biochemistry at the University of Texas, makes it plain that no two of us are alike—far from it! Were everyone identical to you or me, all would perish. It follows that there is no single formula for finding pleasure in aging; my prescription might not work for you. Each of us must seek his own formula, one that is consistent with his *singular* uniqueness. However, the thought of others can light the way to one's own enlightenment.[1]

Whoever would age successfully must not overlook the importance of good health. Years ago I read *The Stress of Life* by Dr. Hans Selye, Université de Montreal—the world's most famous M.D. The lesson? Rid the self of anger, fretting, worry, fear, terror, anxiety about the world going to pot and the like. Dr. Selye presents scientific proof that such emotional experiences generate bodily and life-

---

[1]See *You Are Extraordinary* by Roger J. Williams (New York: Pyramid Books, 1976).

shortening poisons. Be rid of these traumas; look to the good, the encouraging, the light![2]

To find support for the idea that most ills are psychosomatic in origin go back well over two millennia and there it is: "As a man thinketh in his heart, so is he." (Proverbs 23:7) Here is modern support from a doctor specializing in psychosomatic illnesses.

For instance, a patient whose parents have both died of heart disease will be anxious about his own heart. When then a normal diencephalic response to an emotion causes the heart to beat faster or when gastric distension pushes his heart out of its usual position, he will be inclined to interpret what he feels as the beginning of the disease which killed his parents, thinking that he has inherited a weak heart. At once all his fears cluster like a swarm of angry bees on his heart, a vicious cycle is established and thus anxious cortical supervision may eventually lead to organic lesions. He and his family will then be convinced that he did indeed inherit a weak heart, yet this is not at all true.[3]

The above is but one of many illustrations of how death is hastened by fears and other warped emotions. In brief, unless one would speed the deadening process, let him not fear death.

Nothing erases unpleasant thoughts more effectively than conscious concentration on pleasant ones. That is to say, direct the will to focus on the goal that one's emergent energy is designed to accomplish: expanding consciousness.

---

[2](New York: McGraw-Hill Book Company, Inc., 1956).

[3]*Man's Presumptuous Brain* by A. T. W. Simeons, M.D. (New York: E. P. Dutton & Co., 1961).

The mere recognition of this inherent tendency of our nature causes one to concentrate on the positive and to more or less forget the negative side of life. This tends to expand one's mental faculties, which center around the cortex. A noted biologist gives us an interesting sketch of the problem and the hope:

> The normal human brain always contains a greater store of neuroblasts than can possibly develop into neurons during the span of life, and the potentialities of the human cortex are never fully realized. There is a surplus and depending upon physical factors, education, environment, and conscious effort, more or less of the initial store of neuroblasts will develop into mature, functioning neurons. The development of the more plastic and newer tissue of the brain depends to a large extent upon the *conscious efforts* made by the individual. There is every reason to assume that development of cortical functions is promoted by mental activity and that *continued mental activity is an important factor in the retention of cortical plasticity into late life*. Goethe [and others] are among the numerous examples of men whose creative mental activities extended into the years associated with mental decline. There also seem sufficient grounds for the assumption that habitual disuse of these centers results in atrophy or at least brings about a certain mental decline, and examples bearing out this contention are only too numerous.[4]

The above authors provide excellent guidelines if one is to experience the pleasures of aging.

---

[4]See *Fearfully and Wonderfully Made* by Renée von Eulenburg-Wiener (New York: The Macmillan Company, 1938), p. 310.

Let us now reflect on two questions which appear to be relevant to this thesis:

First, who are the greatest contributors to the pleasures of aging?

Second, what tends to bring on atrophy and mental decline?

In the realm of mortal beings, the true nobles—those who light the way—are our gifted tutors, past and present. Few individuals have excelled Goethe in this respect. And I share once more my favorite example of his wisdom:

Nature [Infinite Consciousness or God] understands no jesting; she is always true, always serious, always severe; she is always right, and the errors and faults are always those of man. The man incapable of appreciating her she despises and only to the apt, the pure, and the true, does she resign herself and reveal her secrets.

Also, we can pay homage to ever so many others, including such mentors as Amos Bronson Alcott, Professor Roger J. Williams, Dr. A. T. W. Simeons and Renée von Eulenberg-Wiener.

There is more to the observation of such tutors than first meets the eye. A worthy ambition, they quite correctly imply, is "to die with your boots on" or "go down with your colors flying." For what other reason are we here than to get deeper into life? And if there be any certain key to personal pleasures, it involves the use and development of the faculties—the expanding mind being the most important and, by and large, all that remains for those who are aging.

But there is another reason for looking so favorably on

those who insist on a perpetual striving, an incessant course of training: Each of us has a vested interest in these intellectual noblemen.

We can live our own lives to the fullest only insofar as they dwell among us. The society in which we live—the environment—is conditioned by the absence or presence of those who persistently pursue excellence. The rise and fall of society depends upon this kind of nobility! These tutors are essential to us, and striving to be numbered among them is a worthy effort and aspiration.

Yet, many persons lack any such aspiration. We witness ever so many promising individuals falling by the wayside, stepping away from life, forsaking the effort essential to life's full cycle, just when the process of maturing should begin. Briefly, *the fruit of life abandoned!*

To associate old age with mature judgment is often a mistake, simply because, as Ortega suggested, too many elders react only to external compulsion. The inner development that is prerequisite to maturity tends to terminate too soon, which is why old age, more often than not, is plagued by senility. Yet, the greater the age the richer the maturity, assuming, of course, that the budding process is alive and functioning. In these rare cases, old age and mature judgment go hand in hand, the older the wiser!

If I am not mistaken, freedom is to be expected only in societies distinguished by a significant number of mature and wise men and women. Maturity and wisdom, of the quality required, is reserved to those who retain the budding phenomenon—cortical plasticity—into those years normally associated with physical decline, that is, into the period when maturing of the intellect becomes at least a possibility.

In any event, I am convinced that the type of maturity here in question will never issue among those who, for whatever reason, permit themselves to "die on the vine." Thus, it is of the utmost importance that we reflect on the obstacles to maturity. If they can be identified, we can, hopefully, avoid or overcome them.

This brings us to the second question: What tends to bring on atrophy and mental decline? Obviously, no one knows all the answers. But here is a factor that may be number one: *the retirement syndrome.*

Two forces move millions of people toward retirement as a goal: temptation and compulsion. Many people are congenitally lazy, if not physically, at least mentally. Their mental activities have stagnated, leaving them uninteresting even to themselves, let alone to others; they cannot abide their own company or being alone with their thoughts. They seek merriment and diversion supplied by others. Any excuse, however flimsy, to avoid thinking for self! Such persons have no fruit to ripen, no mental activity to mature.

There are others who have had no thought since early adulthood but to "get it made." By the time that goal is achieved, abstract thought has been too long neglected for reactivation or renewal; half-hearted attempts prove unrewarding, so the temptation is to forswear any conscious effort. Mature thoughts? None!

Ever so many persons of high potential look to a vocation for fame or fortune, and neglect to choose one in harmony with their unique capabilities. As a consequence, the job is likely to be boring; holidays and vacations—little retirements—are highlights of the seasons. As the years pass, full retirement seems more and more attractive; there is no incentive to extend mental activity to its maturity.

The thought of retirement is anathema to me. I have not experienced any of the usual temptations to quit working and, thus, can list only a few of the more obvious examples. But it seems clear that there would be little pressure for compulsory retirement if retirement itself were not a common goal. It seems to add up to this: Let's formalize and legalize that which the vast majority so ardently favor! The following examples of compulsive forces stem from these common temptations.

Retirement, of course, is a relative term. The shortened work week, enforced by edict, is a case in point. One must "retire" week after week—not work beyond the legal forty hours—or the employer will be forced to a higher hourly rate, in effect, a fine.

Legal holidays seem never to be abandoned even after the cause they were meant to celebrate has been forgotten. Instead, there are countless excuses for increasing their number. Minor retirements en masse!

Social security payments are withheld from senior citizens who elect to work and earn. Activity is penalized, inactivity is rewarded.

Governmental unemployment payments often exceed what some persons could earn by working, thus inducing retirement.

Most corporations, educational and religious institutions, chambers of commerce, trade associations, and other organizations compel retirement at 65; many make it attractive to retire at 60; and we hear more and more of retiring at even earlier years. The sole criterion is the number of moons that have come and gone; whether the budding process is dead, or at its peak, is not even considered. As a consequence of this indiscriminate, rule-of-thumb procedure, many of the nation's best men are "put out to pasture."

These illustrations suffice to emphasize the retirement syndrome. It is, today, the common fetish and the end is not in sight. Under these circumstances, it is remarkable that even a few individuals are capable of spontaneous and joyous effort, that is, able to experience the maturing period. No wonder that the perceptive Ortega observed such individuals to "stand out isolated, monumentalized"!

In one sense, it is lamentable that those who have advanced in wisdom and maturity should "stand out isolated, monumentalized." Far better if there were more such persons, making the few less conspicuous than they are. Not everyone will make it, of course, but maturity surely is within the reach of countless thousands at the modest price of conscious, persistent, dedicated, prayerful effort. Realizing one's potentialities, whatever they are, may be the highest reward earthly life has to offer.

That my life still begins with each moment can be assigned in part to a stroke of good fortune—vocation and avocation are identical; *work and pleasure are one and the same.*

In a piece, similar to this one, written at the age of 70, I settled on my retirement policy: Short of effective compulsions to the contrary, I propose to ride my bicycle till I fall off!

Working on behalf of freedom, the pleasures of aging are boundless for me. It is joyous, not tiring, thus, never any retiring!

NAME INDEX